My Beautiful
Daughter

Other books in the growing Faithgirlz!™ library

Bibles

The Faithgirlz! Bible

NIV Faithgirlz! Backpack Bible

Faithgirlz! Bible Studies

Secret Power of Love

Secret Power of Joy

Secret Power of Goodness

Secret Power of Grace

Fiction

From Sadie's Sketchbook

Shades of Truth (Book One)

Flickering Hope (Book Two)

Waves of Light (Book Three)

Brilliant Hues (Book Four)

Sophie's World Series

Sophie's World

Sophie's Secret

Sophie Under Pressure

Sophie Steps Up

Sophie's First Dance

Sophie's Stormy Summer

Sophie's Friendship Fiasco

Sophie and the New Girl

Sophie Flakes Out

Sophie Loves Jimmy

Sophie's Drama

Sophie Gets Real

The Girls of Harbor View

Girl Power (Book One)

Take Charge (Book Two)

Raising Faith (Book Three)

Secret Admirer (Book Four)

The Lucy Series

Lucy Doesn't Wear Pink (Book One)

Lucy Out of Bounds (Book Two)

Lucy's Perfect Summer (Book Three)

Lucy Finds Her Way (Book Four)

Boarding School Mysteries

Vanished (Book One)

Betrayed (Book Two)

Burned (Book Three)

Poisoned (Book Four)

Nonfiction

Faithgirlz! Journal

The Faithgirlz! Handbook

The Faithgirlz! Cookbook

No Boys Allowed

What's a Girl to Do?

Girlz Rock

Chick Chat

Real Girls of the Bible

Faithgirlz! Whatever

My Beautiful Daughter

The Skin You're In

Girl Talk

*Everybody Tells Me to Be Myself
but I Don't Know Who I Am*

Girl Politics

Check out www.Faithgirlz.com

faiThGirLz!™
the beauty of believing

My Beautiful Daughter

What It Means
to Be Loved by God

Tasha K. Douglas

ZONDERkidz
ZONDERVAN.com/
AUTHORTRACKER
follow your favorite authors

ZONDERKIDZ

Faithgirlz! My Beautiful Daughter

Copyright © 2012 by Tasha K. Douglas

This title is also available as a Zondervan ebook.
Visit www.zondervan.com/ebooks

Requests for information should be addressed to:
Zonderkidz, Grand Rapids, Michigan 49530

Library of Congress Cataloging-in-Publication Data

Douglas, Tasha, 1974-
    My beautiful daughter : what it means to be loved by God / by Tasha
Douglas.
        p. cm. — (Faithgirlz)
    ISBN 978-0-310-72643-2 (softcover)
    1. Girls — Religious life — Juvenile literature. 2. Preteens — Religious
life — Juvenile literature. 3. God (Christianity) — Love — Juvenile literature.
4. God (Christianity) — Fatherhood — Juvenile literature. I. Title.
BV4551.3.D68 2012
248.8'2—dc23
                                            2011043730

Any Internet addresses (websites, blogs, etc.) and telephone numbers in this book
are offered as a resource. They are not intended in any way to be or imply an
endorsement by Zondervan, nor does Zondervan vouch for the content of these
sites and numbers for the life of this book.

Cover design: Kris Nelson
Interior design and composition: Greg Johnson, Textbook Perfect

Printed in the United States of America

---

12 13 14 15 16 /DCI/ 22 21 20 19 18 17 16 15 14 13 12 11 10 9 8 7 6 5 4 3 2 1

To my beautiful daughters,

Téa Carise and Tori Nicole

Contents

CHAPTER 1

Recognizing Your Father's Face

I got it!" Briana Robinson leaped from her bed and sprinted to the telephone. Not much longer and she'd have her own cell phone. It was the call she'd anticipated all morning long. In sixteen more hours, she would begin her first day as a seventh-grader at Live Oak Junior High School. It was the biggest day of her life so far. After years of watching her older sister, Ashley, do cool stuff like hosting sleepovers, Briana figured the time had finally come for her to have some fun too.

The consummate fashionista, Briana's idea of fun meant facing life's monumental moments in style. She considered the matter of what to wear on the first day of school a major decision. The incoming call from her best friend, Jessica Moore, would help her make a good one. Briana grabbed the telephone, catching her breath before speaking.

"Hey Jess! What are you wearing tomorrow?"

"I don't know yet. How 'bout you?"

"I'm not sure either."

"Nothing we can't solve with a trip to the mall, right? Do you think your mom would take us?"

"Maybe. She doesn't get home 'til four thirty, though."

"Call her and ask her."

"No, I'm only supposed to call for something serious. She'll call to check on me. Then I'll ask."

"Cool. What are you gonna get?"

"Ashley has a cute pair of jeans that I like. And I know the perfect hoodie to go with 'em."

"Why don't you just borrow Ashley's jeans then?"

"Please. They are so big on me I can't even walk. I'd rather have some skinny jeans anyway. Besides, Mom doesn't let us share clothes."

Briana and Jessica desired to look good. They were glad their school permitted them to wear their own clothing instead of uniforms. In the sixth grade, Briana earned the best-dressed award and her picture in the yearbook. She was determined to keep that status in junior high too. The telephone beeping with another call interrupted her goal-setting daydream.

"Jess, let me get that. It's probably my mom."

"Okay. Call me back when you get done."

"I will." Briana switched calls. "Hey, Mom."

"Hello, Bree. Is that the proper way to answer the telephone?"

"No. But I knew it was you. We do have caller ID, remember?"

"Don't get sassy, Briana Robinson. You still need to answer the phone correctly. You doin' alright?"

"Kinda. Well actually, no. Not really ... Mom?"

"Mmm hmm."

Briana zipped her question out as fast as she could. "Do you think you can take me and Jess to the mall when you get home? I really want to get a hoodie like Ashley's to wear to school tomorrow ... please." She grimaced as she waited for her mother's response.

"Oh, sweetheart, I'm sorry. I have to work late. That's what I was calling to tell you. I'm really sorry, Briana. I promise I'll make it up to you. Anyway, what about all the stuff your grandmother sent you?"

"It's nice. But I want to wear something slammin' on the first day."

"Slamming?"

"You know what I mean, Mom. Something cool. All that stuff Granny got is too babyish."

"I understand. Well, try to find something in your closet just for tomorrow. We're not going to the mall tonight. I won't make it home until six thirty."

With that, Briana's hope of becoming the most popular girl in school began evaporating. Her mother seemed not to care. "Where's Ashley?" she asked.

"She's in her room."

"Let me talk to her please."

"I'll get her."

Briana pushed the hold button and then placed the telephone back on the cradle. She also hung her head, disappointed that her pursuit of popularity was now on hold, and Mom wouldn't take her to the mall. She considered begging, but it was useless. Briana envisioned her mom planting her hands on her hips, with that look on her face. You know the one. It means, *I said no. Now no more whining, and do not ask me again.*

In moments like that, Briana thought about her father.

She gently tapped on Ashley's closed bedroom door. "Mom's on the phone."

Ashley opened the door, noticing the tears slowly filling Briana's brown eyes. "What's wrong?"

Briana shrugged. "Nothin', I'm fine." She turned from her sister, hurrying off to her own bedroom. Closing the bedroom door behind her, she sighed and plopped down at her desk. The huge calendar on top almost completely covered it. It was easy for her to notice the dreaded Saturday date. She had circled it at least a hundred times with a hot pink heart.

Briana had her dress. She had her shoes. And of course, she had her jewelry. There was only one thing she was missing for the Father-Daughter Sweetheart Dance: *her father.* Even though her uncle William would take her as he did every year, the fact that he was not her actual father only made her even sadder.

She understood the importance of being grateful for Uncle William's love and kindness, and she was. Still, knowing all the other girls would be at the dance with their fathers, and that she would not, left Briana feeling empty.

Drumming her fingers on the desk, Briana resolved to make the best of her situation. She thought, oh well, he's not going to magically appear 'cause I'm sitting here tapping this desk. She got up and slowly opened the closet door, as if she were afraid of the clothes inside.

The door creaked, reminding her that everything in her closet was old, and nowhere near good enough to wear on the first day of junior high. She stood there, arms crossed in disappointment, deciding what outfit would have to make do for her debut. "Ugh!" she yelled, slamming the closet door. The wall shelf holding her cheerleading trophies shook. All her awards tumbled to the floor.

The crash alarmed Ashley. She dashed through the door to Briana's room. "What happened?"

"I just closed my closet door too hard. Geez, don't you knock? Calm down."

"If there's something bothering you Briana, you should just say so. What's up?"

Ashley could be a cool big sister at times. When Briana felt like her mother didn't understand, Ashley was willing to listen. "What's up with that," Briana said, "is I'm tired of not having Dad around! Don't you ever wonder why our dad left us and Mom?"

Ashley sat down on Briana's bed and patted the vacant spot beside her with her hand. Briana complied with the request and sat down. "You know, Bree, I used to wonder but not so much anymore. There are times when I miss Dad too. But, I'm learning that adults have a lot of responsibilities.

They have to make choices that we don't even think about yet. Sometimes they make good ones, sometimes they don't. But it doesn't mean they don't love us."

"Yeah. But shouldn't you be with someone if you love them so much?"

Ashley held up her pointer finger, got up from the bed, and walked out of the room. When she came back in, she carried a mustard yellow colored photo album. Sitting down on the bed with Briana, Ashley opened the old album and took out a picture. She showed it to Briana. "Does this look like someone who doesn't love you?"

"Is that baby me?"

"Yes. And that's Dad holding you. Mom told me he had just finished giving you a bath. It was his nightly routine. You would scream when he took off your clothes to get you all cleaned up. But after that, you loved it! He would bathe you, dress you in that goofy looking outfit, and then read you a story before you went to sleep. Every single night."

"How embarrassing!" In the picture, newborn Briana is naked, and her dad is holding her close to his chest, bundled in a white hooded robe with pink rabbit ears and feet. "He looks handsome, don't you think?"

"I guess you could say that. I think he looks proud mostly. Look at that big smile."

"Maybe." She handed the picture back to Ashley. "Guess he wasn't proud enough to stay though."

Before leaving the room, Ashley leaned over and kissed Briana on the forehead. "You keep it."

Making her way back to the closet, Briana stared into the eyes of the man in the picture, a man she hardly knew and had no memory of having seen. She could not recognize her own father's face. In that moment, at first, everything felt unacceptable. Her clothes felt unacceptable. Her life felt unacceptable. She felt utterly unacceptable. Yet, the picture seemed to nag Briana, begging her to stare. The longer she looked, the more she thought that maybe Ashley's story was true. Maybe this man had loved her, cared for her, and wanted her more than she ever knew. "Where are you," she whispered. "Don't you understand how much I need you?"

Thinking her whispers were only unheard words falling to the ground, Briana sank to the floor of her closet. Her heart was sunken too. She started pounding her fists on the floor, angry with Mom for not taking her to the mall, her dad for leaving her, and herself for crying like a baby. Maybe angry with God too, wherever he was.

She took one last jab at the floor, but this time it felt like the floor punched her back! "Ouch!" Briana said. "What was that?" She looked down to see that she had hit her hand on the buckle of a glittery pink belt. Mmm. That's cute, she thought. Briana picked up the belt and studied it, trying to remember the last time she wore it. Then she noticed the price tag dangling from the buckle. Wait a minute, she thought. Have I even worn this belt yet?

That one question led Briana on a style expedition, hunting vigorously through her closet. Just minutes earlier, she'd considered it a wilderness of toxic material destined for a hazardous waste bin. Not anymore. In the middle of her frustration, Briana had discovered first day fashion that would launch her immediately into the Live Oak Junior High hall of fame for fashion! Yes!

Briana's Box

How is a girl supposed to understand what it means to be her father's daughter when he's not even around? It's tough. But understanding what it means to be the much-loved daughter of your father is a huge deal in your life, because it shapes how you think about God, your Father in heaven. What you think of your heavenly Father affects your life more than any other belief you have.

If your dad's not around much, you might feel that Father God is absent when you need him too. That would be totally wrong thinking about God! So, *Faithgirlz!* is here to help you believe that understanding and receiving Father God's love is possible and even more than that— it's actually your future!

The connection you share with Father God matters more than any other relationship you have. The beauty of believing that you are his beautiful daughter means you get to . . .

- Experience a love-filled relationship that lasts forever.
- Expand your family to include all Father God's children.
- Envision the bright future prepared for you by Father God.

Sound good? Then get to it, girl! Start by doing a special Faithgirl assignment called a daughter deed.

Daughter Deed

Do you understand how Briana felt because you miss your father too? Maybe he died when you were too young to remember. Is your father one of the brave people serving our country in the military? Perhaps your mother and father divorced. Does your dad spend so much time working to take care of your family that you two share little time together? Do you, like Briana, whisper, "Where are you," unsure if anyone hears your voice?

Can you do a daughter deed, and share with Briana how you feel about your dad? Take all the time you need, and in the space below write down some of your experiences with your father. If you have any encouraging words for Bree, be sure to write those down too. Let her know what cheers you up when you're feeling down about your dad.

_____

_____

_____

_____

_____

_____

Thanks, Faithgirl. Sometimes it might seem that no one hears you, or even cares about the special thoughts you just shared with Briana. The truth is there is someone who always hears you. He is Father God, and he's been waiting on you. Are you ready to break out of the box and meet him? Then read on! Briana's showing you the beauty of believing and what it means to be loved by God.

Believing with Briana

You can think of Briana's quest for the perfect outfit as a good way of learning how to begin experiencing the love of Father God. Do you remember why Bree ended up staring into her closet in a fashion fog? First, her big sister's jeans were too big for her, and she wanted a narrow, skinny fitting pair. What was the second barricade to Briana earning her best-dressed bragging rights? She had no way of getting to the mall. Right. And the final wake-up call from her fashion fantasy was her mom's injunction against the borrowing of clothing. In the end, whatever Briana was going to wear to school was already in her closet.

In the same way that Briana wanted skinny-fit jeans, you will receive God's love by walking a path that is narrow and focused on him. Also, just as she was unable to depend on anyone else to take her to the mall, you are responsible for your own spiritual journey. Finally, in the same way that Briana submitted to her mom's guideline of no clothes sharing, God's daughters learn to submit to him and obey the guidelines he establishes for your own good. In the end, you too will find everything you need in your closet. You just have to look again and discover what's inside.

The story captured in Briana's photograph with her own dad also pictures the story of Father God's love for you. Just as Briana's dad loved sharing the nightly ritual with his precious daughter, Father God loves doing special things for you. His desire is to love you so well that he irresistibly draws you to loving him right back and trusting him with your life!

Love the Lord your God with all your heart and with all your soul and with all your mind. This is the first and greatest commandment.
— *Matthew 22:37–38*

Like Briana's dad, Father God has a special way of lavishing his love on his daughters. You know that Father God loves you, his beautiful daughter, because he tenderly ...

- Cleans you
- Clothes you
- Calms you

Has anyone ever told you how a newborn baby looks? It is a grimy sight at first! Before wrapping you in a toasty warm blanket, dressing you in cute infant clothing, and presenting you to your anxiously awaiting family, health care professionals washed off the messy residue caused by your previous life inside your mother's womb. That first bath, though, was only one of many. It started a practice of regular washing that would keep you healthy and clean for the rest of your life.

As a baby, you needed help keeping clean. As you grew older, someone taught you what to do, and you were able to wash yourself off regularly, keeping yourself clean on your own. And even though you know what to do now, sometimes the mess gets so big, you need help getting cleaned up.

In Briana's family, her dad was the one who enjoyed washing his daughter. Father God loves washing his daughters too! Just like that newborn baby, when you're first born into God's family, all the grubbiness of your life before you knew him clings to you. Messy birth was a part of being born into your family. It's also a part of being born into the family of Father God.

Surely I was sinful at birth, sinful from the time my mother conceived me.

— Psalm 51:5

Yet, God never intends to leave you icky! Like Bree's father, it pleases him to wash you clean when dirty situations start to pollute your life. When you're not in the best of moods, your parents don't seem to understand, or if your friends start treating you unkindly, your Father in heaven will wash you clean.

As you grow to know him more and more, God will teach you to keep yourself clean. And yes, there will be those times when, although you are all grown up, you still need help getting cleaned!

When you bathe, what do you do after drying off? You put some clothes on! After all, it's chilly, right? Knowing his baby daughter was unable to dress herself, Briana's dad clothed her, keeping her protected from the harsh elements—the heat or the cold—of her surroundings. Ashley thought the outfit Briana's dad chose looked ridiculous. Still, Briana was held close and snuggled by her father, wearing a white rabbit-eared robe as a sign of her father's great love for her.

Father God has great love for you, and he too loves clothing you, knowing you're unable to do it yourself. His desire is to cover and protect you from the harsh experiences that inevitably you will encounter in life. At times, life's pressures make you feel like your heart is being scorched! Other times, situations may seem so cold and dismal that your heart begins to freeze up on you. In those times, remember what it means to be Father God's daughter. No matter how ridiculous it seems to anyone else, it means he's intimately covering you in relationship with him, and you're protected.

Wouldn't you be ready to get some rest after being all toasty in your cute white robe? Well, yeah! Briana's dad knew she was too. That's why the last thing he used to do was softly tell her a story so she could go to bed and rest peacefully. After a long day of drooling, babbling, scooting, eating, and napping—all the tasks of hardworking babies everywhere he understood that she needed some rest. He lulled Briana into calmness with the sound of his voice, giving her peace and rest from her work.

Father God also softly speaks to you, his daughter, knowing that when you focus on his voice, it calms you, gives you peace, and makes you rest. After all the hard work that you do—studying for school, your responsibilities in your home, serving with your club, and hanging with your friends—God wants you to make time to restore all that energy you've expended!

Praise Prompt

Psalm 23 is a favorite song of many of God's daughters. It shares all the wonderful things Father God does because he loves his children so much. Think about this song, and express your gratitude to Father God however you like. You can dance, sing, clap, or even write your own melody!

Psalm 23
The Lord is my shepherd, I lack nothing.
He makes me lie down in green pastures,
he leads me beside quiet waters,
he refreshes my soul.
He guides me along the right paths
for his name's sake.
Even though I walk
through the darkest valley,
I will fear no evil,
for you are with me;
your rod and your staff,
they comfort me.
You prepare a table before me
in the presence of my enemies.

You anoint my head with oil;
my cup overflows.
Surely your goodness and love will follow me
all the days of my life,
and I will dwell in the house of the Lord
forever.

Don't you just love praising God? He so deserves it! Now, let's take a closer look at how Briana learned the beauty of believing, and you can too. Like brilliant gemstones, Briana's tidbits are principles of great value to help you understand what it means to be God's beautiful daughter. As you grow to recognize your heavenly Father, your journey will include ...

@ Intentionality   @ Seeking
@ Intimacy   @ Seeing
@ Submission

Briana's Tidbit #1: Intentionality

As much as Briana liked her sister Ashley's jeans, she was unable to wear them because they were too big. Bree's preference was for narrow, skinny jeans that complement a girl her size. That's a great choice! The way to finding Father God is a bit like wearing a pair of great fitting skinny jeans. It's narrow. You'll begin to experience God's love as you intentionally focus on him, and then walk in the way he directs you. Make it your single purpose to focus on God, and you will enter into a life of love with him.

Enter through the narrow gate. For wide is
the gate and broad is the road that leads to
destruction, and many enter through it. But small
is the gate and narrow the road that leads to life,
and only a few find it.

— Matthew 7:13–14

Briana's Tidbit #2: Intimacy

It bummed Briana out that she had no one to take her and Jessica to the mall. Unable to drive herself yet, she was dependent on adults to take her places. Briana learned a valuable lesson though. She realized she had to limit her dependence on other people. She could only occasionally count on others to take her where she wanted to go. The same is true for you, daughter. You still need other people to help you grow into your love walk with Father God. Yet, you won't always depend on other people to take you where you want to go in your relationship with him. You will walk with God in the company of other daughters and sons, and you will definitely need help from your brothers and sisters along the way. Still, being loved by God means having your own personal bond with him that carries you to the special, secret place only the two of you share.

Briana's Tidbit #3: Submission

Sometimes Briana thinks her mom's rules make little sense. Seriously, what's wrong with borrowing a cute jacket or sweater from Jessica or Ashley? Despite her own opinion though, she does what her mom tells her to do. Okay. She does what her mom tells her to do most of the time! That's because in her heart Briana believes her mom only wants good things to happen in her life. Even when she disagrees with her mom's plans at first, they always seem to work out for Briana in the end. So she's learned to smile in her heart because her mom's only looking out for her best interests. After smiling on the inside, she follows Mom's directions.

In the same way that Briana yields to her mom's plans for her, being loved by Father God means that you yield to his plans for you. Sometimes God's thoughts are senseless to you. It's because his thoughts are higher than yours! As his daughter, though, you can trust that his plans for you are good.

> **"For I know the plans I have for you," declares the Lord, "plans to prosper you and not to harm you, plans to give you hope and a future."**
>
> *—Jeremiah 29:11*

When you agree to do things God's way because you understand how much he loves you, he works things out so they turn out good for you, just as they did for Briana.

> **And we know that in all things God works for the good of those who love him, who have been called according to his purpose.**
>
> *—Romans 8:28*

Daughter, You Decide

What do you do when you disagree with your parents or other leaders in your life? How do you feel when they ask you to do things and you don't understand why? Do you do exactly what you are directed to do immediately and with a smile inside your heart?

Briana's Tidbit #4: Seeking

After pillaging her closet, Bree learned that often the purpose of a problem is to help you make unlikely discoveries in unlikely places. She didn't know she had amazing outfits yet to be worn stashed right in her very own closet! Fashion success, present the entire time! And to think it all started on her closet floor with one simple question.

That's part of how it starts for you too. When you find your closet, your secret place of talking alone with God, you discover this about what it means to be loved by God: he's given you everything you need to face any challenge in life—and win! That doesn't mean you won't face challenges. You will. It's a fact of life. But you can trust God is with you through everything. What you're looking for is inside of you!

> Then you will call on me and come and pray to me, and I will listen to you. You will seek me and find me when you seek me with all your heart.
>
> Jeremiah 29:12–13

You're really on your way to discovering the hidden treasure Father God has for you when you start asking him questions. Like Briana, you may think he doesn't hear you, but he does. He will answer. Maybe not in exactly the way you want, but God is able to see the big picture, and he will provide for you in the best way he sees fit.

Ask and it will be given to you; seek and you will find; knock and the door will be opened to you. For everyone who asks receives; the one who seeks finds; and to the one who knocks, the door will be opened.

— Matthew 7:7–8

Briana's Tidbit #5: Seeing

Do you remember Briana returning the photo of her and her father to Ashley? She really didn't want to keep it. Briana had difficulty believing her father loved her or wanted her. She questioned her dad's love because she'd never seen him before. It's hard to trust someone you've never even seen! Yet, as Ashley told her the story of how much her father loved her, her thoughts about her dad started changing. The longer she stared at the picture, the more her way of thinking about her father—and herself—shifted. With each fresh glance, she had a new vision of who her dad really was, and even though she couldn't see him, she believed that he loved her.

As it was with Briana, so it is with you and Father God. Receiving Father God's love is mind-boggling! Trust the love of someone invisible to you? Yeah, right. But that's exactly what faith is all about—the beauty of believing!

Now faith is confidence in what we hope for and assurance about what we do not see.

— *Hebrews 11:1*

How's that supposed to happen for you? Just like it did for Bree as she heard the story of the picture with her father. You'll experience the beauty of believing as you hear the story of God's love for you, over and over again. The more you hear it, the clearer the image you have of him becomes. With each new glance, you'll look at and think differently about God, and yourself, than you already do, until at last, you've got it! The more you open yourself up to him, trust him with your life and decisions, the more he will reveal himself to you. You're loving and looking toward Father God by faith—to lead you in your life, help you make decisions, and trusting that he is with you (and he is). That is faith! Remember, you are God's beautiful daughter!

Aren't you? Maybe reading all of this is causing you to look at your situation differently. Are you ready to love and look toward Father God through faith? Are you ready to hear Father God call you? Then it's time to make that step toward your beginning.

Beginnings with Briana

Oh, wait! There's one detail remaining in Briana's story about her dad. She thought it was totally embarrassing, remember? Ashley said it made Briana scream at the top of her lungs! No one likes being exposed, but before he could bathe her, Briana's dad had to make her a bit uncomfortable and remove her clothing.

You see, before Father God can clean up the messiness of life, he has to remove everything that's covering it up. That means helping you to see what might be hovering over you, around you, like smog. Maybe it's placing too much time into worrying how other's think of you, wondering if you are "cool" in their eyes. Are you trying to be a girl that fits into the "world"? As God's daughter, you have an inner beauty, an inner light to show to the world. But sometimes the light has to be cleaned before it can put forth its brilliant shine. Sure, nakedness can be uncomfortable, but the discomfort is temporary. The pleasure of being cleaned, clothed, and calmed in connection with Father God lasts forever and blows those bare-skinned moments to smoke!

So go ahead and scream if you want, but just be honest with God. Let him know exactly how you feel. Seriously, he already knows what's in your heart anyway! By sharing and keeping it real with God, you invite him to become a part of your world, like a friend. The more you talk and share, just like with any friend, the closer you become. Then you'll recognize his voice that's been inviting you to become a part of his all along.

Daughter, Declare Your Prayer!

Father, thank you for your love! Lead me to your banquet hall, where your sign over me is love. For many waters cannot quench love, and rivers cannot sweep it away. You are making me see and think about things the way you do, and I'm glad. I want to love and look to you through faith. Please, show yourself to me.

CHAPTER 2

Respecting Your Father's Favorite

Lunchtime is Briana's favorite hour of the day. When she's with her friends, their stories about the morning's activities fill her up. That, plus the freshly baked banana-nut muffins the cafeteria lady makes every day!

Bree's third period social studies classroom is right around the corner from the cafeteria, and around 11:30 the smell of those muffins made her stomach grumble in expectation. She rushed through the food line, heading straight for the designated lunch table where Jessica and the rest of the cheer squad were waiting. That's when she saw him.

The sight of Austin Thomas suddenly made Briana feel more like hurling than eating.

"What's up, Butterfingers?" he said. "Don't drop your tray like you do the basketball." He made an exaggerated gesture like she was going to cover him with her milk.

"Go away, Austin."

He followed her to their table. "I'm just saying. You seem to have a hard time holding on to stuff."

The girls strategically chose where to sit. From the back of the cafeteria, they could monitor everyone. The rear location was also the only spot that allowed them to peek out the large window to the outside commons area. From there, they could admire the football players sitting under the massive live oak tree planted in the middle of the commons. Every year, new football players carved their name and number into the sturdy, wide trunk. It was their way of connecting with the title-winning champions of the past who played for the Live Oak Lions.

Besides that, the school board had approved the installation of new lighting meant to brighten up the aging space. Until the workers completed the job, their window seat preference was the best-lit and illuminated place in the cafeteria—perfect for "people-peepin'," as Briana called it.

Jessica noticed how irritated Briana was with Austin's unrequested escort. "Well, she has no problem holding on to you though, does she? I'm going to start calling you 'Tag-a-long Thomas' since you can't seem to get enough of my girl. From now on, if you want to talk to her, make sure you go through me first, Tag-a-long." Briana and Jess fist bumped.

People admired Bree and Jessica's relationship. They met when they were seven years old, when their families moved into the neighborhood at the same time.

Their neighbor, Mrs. Jenkins, hosted a barbeque in her backyard to welcome them. With an awesome swimming pool in the backyard, she had the best house on the block. It's the perfect spot to endure the sweltering summer heat. The day of the party, the two girls wore the exact same bathing suit! Bree knew that any girl who would pick the same water wear had to be wonderful. Through cheerleading camps, youth group, retreats, big sisters, and baby brothers, they've been besties since day one! Briana and Jessica love each other, and they don't take kindly to insults.

Bree sat down next to Jessica, and Austin bent over to whisper in Briana's ear. "Just a helpful hint. You catch the ball first, then you take off and dribble with it." He stood up and made catch and dribble motions with his hands. All the guys at the other end of the table laughed.

"Catch this!" Bree yelled. She elbowed Austin in his stomach.

The sound of her angry voice drew the attention of Mrs. Gray, one of the seventh grade English teachers. Mrs. Gray walked over to their table, "Is there a problem Miss Robinson?"

"Yes. Allow me to introduce you." Smiling, Briana extended her hand toward Austin. "Mrs. Gray, meet Problem."

Everybody laughed, even Austin.

"What's going on you two?"

"Austin's making fun of me because I messed up in gym class!"

"Is that true?" Mrs. Gray looked at Austin.

"No," he said.

"Okay, but, it was just a joke," Austin confessed.

"So you've got jokes, is that it? How does Coach Sanders feel about all those jokes? Doesn't he like to be notified when his comical basketball players, such as yourself, crack one joke too many?"

He looked at Briana. "My bad." Smiling, he tapped her on the shoulder. "I'm sorry. I was just playing around." He extended his hand for her to shake. "Are we cool?"

Briana shook his hand as briefly as possible. "Whatever." She looked at the teacher. "Thank you, Mrs. G."

"That's why I'm here." She patted Briana on the shoulder. "It's my job to keep you out of trouble." She looked toward Austin. "Now finish your lunch before it's time to go."

Briana sat back down and resumed her conversation with her friends while they finished eating. When only five minutes remained until the start of the next lunch period, the crowded cafeteria quickly thinned. The mass exodus of students leaving the cafeteria collided with the

Daughter, You Decide

What do you do when someone makes jokes about you? How do you feel when they attempt to gain laughs at your expense? Do you return the insult and make jokes about them?

famished group attempting to enter. Can you say, major chaos?

"I never have understood why we're not allowed to use the other door to get in here," Jessica said.

"The problem is not that there's only one way in," said Briana. "The problem is the people who don't get the plan and follow directions."

Jessica surveyed the long line of students trying to exit through the entrance. "You mean people like your boy Austin?"

Briana saw Austin standing in the line, knuckling Nicholas's arm. "First of all, he's not my boy. Second of all, right. People exactly like Austin. They just don't understand what's up."

"I'm sure he wouldn't mind if you showed him the way," Jessica said, winking.

"What's that supposed to mean?" Briana felt her face heating up.

"It's so obvious, Bree. He likes you."

"Yeah, right. The only way I care to show Austin Thomas is back to California where he came from."

"Don't be so hard on him. You know he's cute. And smart too. He's probably still just trying to figure things out, you know what I mean? They've only been here since the summer. It's basically like he's starting a brand new life. You wouldn't know what to do either."

"Maybe. But this is not that serious. And I can't believe you're sticking up for him and not me, by the way!" She pointed to the cafeteria's entrance. "That door is for coming in." She turned and pointed to the cafeteria's exit. "That door is for leaving. Notice the prominent sign that says *exit* in big … red … letters. Duh! If he's so smart, why can't he read the signs?"

"Wow. I knew it! You like him too! But I didn't know you liked him that much," Jessica said.

Briana's Box

You've probably been called something other than your name, just like Austin called Briana "Butterfingers." How did that make you feel? If it was a name meant to highlight a weakness or shortcoming of yours, like "Butterfingers" in Bree's case, you were likely hurt and angered by it. Here's why.

Names are special. Father God honored Adam, the first human being, with the responsibility of naming every living creature.

> Now the Lord God had formed out of the ground all the wild animals and all the birds in the sky. He brought them to the man to see what he would name them; and whatever the man called each living creature, that was its name.
>
> — *Genesis 2:19*

Names make up our identity. Yet your name goes beyond simple identification of you as a person. To Father God, your name represents *you*. In the Bible, there are many stories of families naming their children based on the experiences the family had in bringing that child into the world.

> **So in the course of time Hannah became pregnant and gave birth to a son. She named him Samuel, saying, "Because I asked the Lord for him."**
> — *1 Samuel 1:20*

The name Briana means "noble". Her parents chose that name for her because they envisioned their daughter as a woman of honor and dignity. When others negatively refer to you instead of using your name, it hurts because your name suggests who you are as a young woman.

Daughter Deed

Do you know what your name means? Can you do a daughter deed, and research the meaning of your name? Start by asking your parents. You will learn a lot about yourself, and you'll have fun doing it too! Be sure to write down what you find out in the space below. You'll want to keep your notes forever!

_____

_____

_____

_____

_____

_____

Praise Prompt

Name-calling is just uncool. When people call you names and say bad things about you, it can really stress you out. Instead of stressing, read and think about the words below from Psalm 139. When you're finished, go stand in front of a mirror. Then look at yourself, and say "I am who Father God says I am! He made me marvelously! Thank you, Father!" And, Faithgirl, make sure you say it loud and proud!

Psalm 139:13–18

For you created my inmost being;
you knit me together in my mother's womb.
I praise you because I am fearfully and wonderfully made;
your works are wonderful,
I know that full well.
My frame was not hidden from you
when I was made in the secret place,
when I was woven together in the depths of the earth.
Your eyes saw my unformed body;
all the days ordained for me were written in your book
before one of them came to be.
How precious to me are your thoughts, God!
How vast is the sum of them!
Were I to count them,
they would outnumber the grains of sand—
when I awake, I am still with you.

Believing with Briana

Now that you understand the significance of names to Father God, are you curious about the name of God himself? Well, grab something to take a few notes because there is much to learn! God's nature is so big and full that you cannot understand everything about who God is with just one name. Throughout history, God has shared many different names for himself with the people who love him. For girls like you who want to know what it means to be loved by God, two connected names mean the most.

The first name comes from a conversation between God and a man named Moses. Moses was a great leader who God directed to free Hebrew people from slavery. Like you, Moses was curious about God's name. Moses knew that the purpose of naming exceeds identification, and lets you know the nature of a person or thing. So, Moses asked God his name. The answer God gave Moses will help you learn a lot about who God is and how you can know him for yourself. Listen in on the conversation between God and Moses:

> Moses said to God, "Suppose I go to the Israelites and say to them, 'The God of your fathers has sent me to you,' and they ask me, 'What is his name?' Then what shall I tell them?"

> God said to Moses, "I AM WHO I AM. This is what you are to say to the Israelites: 'I AM has sent me to you.'"

> God also said to Moses, "Say to the Israelites, 'The LORD, the God of your fathers—the God of Abraham, the God of Isaac and the God of Jacob—has sent me to you.' This is my name forever, the name you shall call me from generation to generation."

Can you imagine asking someone their name and they answer with "I am"? What would you think of them? Maybe you'd be tapping your foot, waiting for them to finish their sentence thinking, okay, so you were saying ... you are? Thankfully, Jesus Christ came along and clarified the fuzziness of the "I AM" answer! It is his name and character that is the most special and highly regarded name to Father God. That name of Jesus Christ deserves more respect than any other name. Here's why.

Has anyone ever told you that you look and act like one of your parents? Maybe you've heard that you have your father's nose, or you walk and talk like your mother. This is because you inherited your physical attributes from your parents. You have a chemical in your body called deoxyribonucleic acid, or DNA for short. DNA is what determines how you look and behave. The reason you resemble your parents is that you have the same DNA they do.

Spiritually speaking, Jesus Christ looks just like his father too! Just as your parents passed down their DNA to you, Father God passed down his DNA to his unique Son, Jesus Christ. Jesus Christ has the exact nature and character of Father God. In fact, Jesus even told his first followers that

"Anyone who has seen me has seen the Father."
—*John 14:9*

Though God the Father is invisible, Jesus Christ the Son is visible. By looking at this Son, Jesus, you can see exactly what God the Father is like.

But, there's a little more to this Jesus looks like his father thing! Not only does Jesus look like the Father, he is actually one with the Father. That's why Jesus could say, if you've seen me, then you've seen the Father. When you wonder what God the Father is like, you can discover him by focusing on Jesus Christ.

Then Jesus cried out, "Whoever believes in me does not believe in me only, but in the one who sent me. The one who looks at me is seeing the one who sent me.

—John 12:44–45

Jesus spoke the words "I AM" too. Just as Father God said the words "I AM" when he talked to Moses, Jesus spoke the words "I AM" frequently as he shared his life with and taught his followers his ways. Jesus shared with his followers that whatever he said is just what the Father told him to say.

On seven special occasions, Jesus said "I AM," and his words make it clear that Jesus is the one who leads daughters to Father God. Now, take a close look at Jesus's statements. Remember, these tidbits are principles of great value to help you understand what it means to be loved by God, and exactly how you can find Father God for yourself! Jesus said:

I am the bread of life.

—John 6:35

I am the light of the world.

—John 8:12

I am the gate.

— *John 10:9*

I am the good shepherd.

— *John 10:14*

I am the resurrection and the life.

— *John 11:25*

I am the way and the truth and the life.

— *John 14:6*

I am vine; you are the branches.

— *John 15:5*

Briana's Tidbit #1: I Am the Bread of Life

Do you remember what fills Briana up at lunchtime besides hanging with her friends? That's right! Those freshly baked banana-nut muffins in the cafeteria. Even though her appetite is small, Briana understands the importance of healthy eating habits to give her body the energy it needs to function at its best. Grainy foods, like Briana's favorite muffins, are those made from wheat, rice, oats, cornmeal, barley, or other cereal grains.

Grains are an important part of a healthy diet because they provide many nutrients you need every day such as fiber, vitamins, and minerals. If you're anything like your bread-loving friend Briana, you know this for sure: when you eat bread, a muffin, or a bowl of brown rice, it fills you up for a long time!

It's the fiber in bread that makes you feel full. Fiber also lowers the chance that you'll ever have heart disease, and it helps your body eliminate waste. The vitamins in grains, especially vitamin B, help your body release stored up energy and keep your brain sharp. The minerals found in grains, like iron and magnesium, help your body carry oxygen in the blood and build up your bones.

Now do you see why Jesus said, "I am the bread of life"? God is loaded with the goodness you need to experience a satisfying life, every day! He is the source of the daily spiritual nutrition you need. Just like eating foods loaded with dietary fiber, when you take God in, he keeps the cares of life from contaminating your heart with disease. When you mistakenly make bad choices and even purposely do things you know are wrong, it's a sign that your heart is unhealthy. In those times, remember that your Father is like fiber! If you make a step to reach out to him, he'll reach out for you, too, and keep your heart healthy.

Just like the vitamin B found in foods from the grain group, God gives you energy and helps your mind stay sharp and focused on the work he needs you to do. That's right, Faithgirl! God's daughters have work to do—and that means you! Your relationship with him gives you the strength of body and mind you need to get the job done well. You may have days when you feel tired and sluggish, or you think you're unable to do something you know you're supposed to do—like homework or soccer practice perhaps! Tell yourself, my Father is like fiber! Then get to it!

> **I became a servant of this gospel by the gift of God's grace given me through the working of his power.**
> *— Ephesians 3:7*

> **For the Spirit God gave us does not make us timid, but gives us power, love and self-discipline.**
> *— 2 Timothy 1:7*

Lastly, God is just like those minerals found in the grainy breads Briana enjoys so much. The iron from grain group foods is critical in helping oxygen stick to the blood that flows through your body. Think of iron as the glue that holds everything together. It's a really big deal if your body lacks the iron to make the oxygen bind to your blood. Every single system, organ, and cell in your body must have oxygen to function normally—and that means you need your iron, Faithgirl.

You also need God. He's just like that iron too. God is the glue that holds everything together so that you can get out there and take action like his strong daughter! With God, all things are possible.

Speaking of strong, how much strength would you have without a sturdy skeleton? You got it. Not so much. The magnesium in Bree's bread keeps your bones tough enough to support you. Guess what, Faithgirl? Your relationship with Father God does the same thing for you. When you're with God, you can celebrate because he's strong and tough enough to support you no matter what challenges or obstacles you have to stand up to each day.

Now it is God who makes both us and you stand firm in Christ.

— 2 Corinthians 1:21

Are you excited yet? If you're like Briana and you spend little time with your dad, you might feel unsure. That's understandable. After all, the whole father thing hasn't worked out that well for you in the past, right? Well, believe this, Faithgirl. Father God created a special place in your heart that is only for him. He is the only one who can fill you with the love and acceptance your heart wants.

Is it possible that you are trying other things or relationships to fill what only Father God can? If you've begun sexually intimate relationships with others, started using drugs and alcohol with some of your friends, or you treat people around you harshly, it might be because you're missing the Father's love.

Daughter Deed

Can you think of anything in your own life that you are using to fill you up instead of your relationship with Father God? Can you do a daughter deed, and write a list of things that you turn to instead of him?

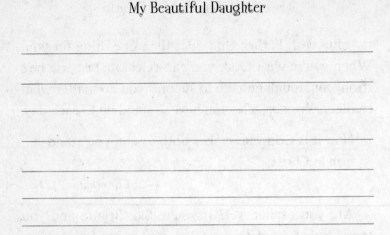

Thanks for being brave. It takes a lot of courage to own up to it when you've been heading in the wrong direction. But you took the first step, which was admitting you've got some changing to do. G-double O-D-J-O-B! Good job, good job! Now, let's get back to Briana's tidbits to learn more about what Father God is all about!

Briana's Tidbit #2: I Am the Light of the World

Do you remember why Bree, Jessica, and the squad chose to sit in the back of the cafeteria?

That's right! They wanted to be able to see what's going on with everybody else! But that wasn't the only reason, right? Remember, the huge window in the back of the cafeteria allows the sunshine in. The sun's radiance illuminates the large room, making it easy for the girls to see what's up in the world of Live Oak—at least among the people who have second lunch like Briana! Also the sunshine helps light the cafeteria itself, which feels dark while new lighting is installed. Lastly, the heat of the sun beaming through the window prevents the frigid cafeteria air from freezing Briana's limbs to icicles!

Jesus said, "I am the light of the world." His words are your reminder that God is like that sunshine bursting through the cafeteria window. As you learned from Briana, the light of the sun helps you see. Light also brightens dark places and it keeps you warm. As his daughter, you can count on Father God to help you see, to displace darkness in the world around you, and to keep you from growing cold.

God enables you to see the way on your path through life. Do you ever feel like your life is a maze? As you're learning, life is full of unexpected twists and turns. Sometimes the decisions you make—which club to join, if you should borrow the money you need for those jeans, if you should go to the dance, or how hard to study for the next test—get overwhelming, and you are unsure of what to do. In those instances, remember that God is light, and he will help you see the best way to walk out of your situation.

God is also the light whose radiance transforms dark places and situations in the world around you. How do you feel when you read about current events or watch the news on television? Do the stories make you sad sometimes? It may be difficult to do at first, but make a decision to focus on the good news, instead of the bad. Here's the good news: even in the middle of the sad and dark circumstances of the world around you, the light of God continues to rise and shine around you because you are his daughter.

> **Arise, shine, for your light has come, and the glory of the Lord rises upon you. See, darkness covers the earth and thick darkness is over the peoples, but the Lord rises upon you and his glory appears over you. Nations will come to your light, and kings to the brightness of your dawn.**
>
> — *Isaiah 60:1–3*

Besides helping you see and overcome darkness, God's light also helps keep you warm.

Have you ever dissed anyone else? Usually it's because they treated you badly first, right? When Briana was cold toward Austin, it was because he'd called her "Butterfingers", remember? Because he's the light of the world, what God does in situations such as Briana's is warm your heart up so you can forgive the person who hurt you. Instead of reacting with a cold heart, the light of his love inside you will motivate you to let go of hurtful words and actions against you.

Briana's Tidbit #3: I Am the Door

Briana allowed Austin's hurtful words to freeze her heart up toward him. Do you remember the conversation she had about him with Jessica? Harsh, don't you think? Being new to Live Oak, Austin still needed help learning the order of things, like which doors to use in the cafeteria. He was ignorant of which door granted access into the room, and that there was only one door students were permitted to use for entering.

Just as the one door used for entering the cafeteria, Jesus Christ is the only door for entering a loving relationship with Father God. Jesus Christ is the person who gives you access to Father God. Since Jesus is God's special son, as God's daughter you can consider Jesus your awesome big brother who leads you to your Father!

At first, this might be a tough idea for you or other people in your life to understand. But, it's like what Briana told Jessica about understanding the plan and following directions. Bree's school officials established a specific point of access into the cafeteria because they wanted to maintain a peaceful environment during the lunch hour. Teachers like Mrs. Gray on duty, the flow of the food lines, and yes, the door through which students enter were all designed to uphold a unique atmosphere, without confusion, in the cafeteria.

Father God desires a peaceful environment too. Seriously, think about how many times you've heard a grown-up talk about how much they just want some peace and quiet! To be honest, sometimes you want that too. What about after a long day of practice? Think about how you feel after wracking your brain over that last math test. Or what about when you came home from that trip to the fair or amusement park? You were ready to lay it down and rest peacefully, girl!

To keep the peace of his environment, Father God had to establish certain guidelines, just as those in the cafeteria. One major disruption to the peace God so loves occurs when his daughters misunderstand or forget that he wants them to live special lives committed to him. These unfortunate memory lapses lead to God's daughters making bad choices and experiencing unpleasant consequences! You remember from the last chapter that God wants his daughters to learn to stay clean, don't you? But he knows that because you are human, sometimes you're going to make messes.

Still, he wants to enjoy being with you! Wanting to enjoy his peaceful environment and the presence of his children, Father God thought of a plan that would accomplish both at the same time. His Son, Jesus Christ, is at the center of that plan. Jesus is the entry point of knowing Father God. He chose Jesus because he is the one son who is able to exist perfectly—without any misjudgments, mistakes, errors, or sin—just as the Father does himself.

So keep the peace, and hit the door, Faithgirl!

Briana's Tidbit #4: I Am the Good Shepherd

Briana liked junior high much better than fifth grade. She felt the teachers treated the students with more respect, like they weren't babies anymore. For example, some of the cafeteria rules in elementary school were different from those in junior high. At Live Oak, students could sit wherever they chose, rather than in assigned seats. One thing that did not change, though, was the presence of teachers in the cafeteria serving lunch duty.

Teachers like Mrs. Gray were essential to keeping cafeteria confusion to a minimum. Do you remember what other duties Mrs. Gray told Briana were a part of her job during lunchtime? Yep, you got it! Mrs. Gray said she was there to protect Briana and to keep her from involvement in troublesome situations.

School cafeterias can be one crazy place, right? When Jesus said, "I am the good shepherd," he was telling you that he serves you in the same way as Mrs. Gray does on cafeteria duty. Jesus is your source of protection and guidance as you go through potentially dangerous environments. When you find yourself involved in the middle of an unpleasant experience, like Briana's exchange with Austin, remember, God's got your back!

One of the main jobs of a shepherd is to keep the sheep he tends from danger. Wouldn't it be nice if you could see everything and know exactly when some situation was about to harm you? The truth is, that's humanly impossible. It is possible for God though. He can see you no matter where you are. He also sees and understands the things that are headed your way—both good and bad. Like a good shepherd, he works to prevent you from putting yourself in harm's way because you can't see what's coming.

But, what about if it's too late, and harm is encroaching? Well, he's there in that instance too. It's a fact of life that sometimes a girl needs rescuing from unplanned disasters! God, the good shepherd, will be there, just like Mrs. Gray was for Briana, to help you out of your miserable situation.

One of the reasons why sheep stay out of danger is they know and trust the voice of their shepherd. This is very important for you too, Faithgirl. As you grow, you will learn when God is speaking to your heart, just as a sheep knows the voice of its shepherd. It is critical that you learn to recognize and trust his voice. He speaks to give you words of direction that will help you stay out of trouble.

> **"His sheep follow him because they know his voice. But they will never follow a stranger; in fact, they will run away from him because they do not recognize a stranger's voice."**
>
> —*John 10:4–5*

Briana's Tidbit #5: I Am the Resurrection and the Life

Because he hurt her feelings, Briana was unhappy with Austin, to say the least! Jessica suggested that Briana consider forgiving him. Do you remember the reason why Jessica thought Austin was unfamiliar with the cafeteria rules? Girl, you're good! Austin and his family were new in town.

If you've ever relocated to a different city or state, you

know how tough it can be packing up and heading out. It takes courage to change communities. You have to adjust to a new climate, new people, and a new way of doing things. As Jessica said, moving from one place to a different one means major change!

Being the new kid on the block is challenging, but it can also be fun. Transition from old experiences to new ones are a part of life, Faithgirl—like Briana graduating from elementary school to junior high. As tough as it might be at first, if you approach a new beginning with the right attitude, it can be rewarding for you.

New life is exactly what Jesus was talking about when he said, "I am the resurrection and the life." With this statement, Jesus was saying that following him leads you to a new way of existing and living. When you recognize that Jesus picked you to become a part of the love between him and Father God, you choose whether to participate. If you say yes, your life as you know it will change drastically, for sure! Yet, new life in the city with Jesus is always better than the life you leave behind!

New life with Jesus means your community of friends will change. You will lose some old friends along the way, but God will replace them with new friends who are also walking with Jesus Christ into the love of Father God. When you are Father God's daughter and a sister of Jesus Christ, your environment changes. Physically, you are still earthbound, of course! Yet, your thinking and your heart are with Jesus Christ.

**Since, then, you have been raised with Christ,
set your hearts on things above, where Christ is,
seated at the right hand of God. Set your minds on
things above, not on earthly things. For you died,
and your life is now hidden with Christ in God.**

— *Colossians 3:1–3*

In your new life with Jesus Christ, you learn to live in a way that is different from your old life. Every town, city, and state has its own unique way of doing things. For example, in some cities you can ride a bus for transportation. Some cities have curfews for youth. While some locations have mayors to help govern, smaller towns have managers. Each location has its own pattern.

God has a pattern for your life too. When you receive new life from Jesus Christ, day by day, he makes your mind new by shaping it to God's pattern, instead of the old one to which you were accustomed. Before too long, he has transformed you, and the life you once knew no longer exists!

You might be thinking, well, what's so wrong with the life I have right now? Perhaps things are going well for you, and there is little you want to change. That's fantastic, Faithgirl. God is good to people who receive the new life of his Son, Jesus Christ, and to those who do not receive him. A life overflowing with God's goodness, though, is an exclusive benefit of those who choose to follow Jesus Christ to Father God. What will you choose? Keep on reading for more tidbits to help you decide.

Briana's Tidbit #6: I Am the Way and the Truth and the Life

The unfolding events of the mild altercation between Briana, Austin, and Mrs. Gray contain great information to help you understand what Jesus meant by saying, "I am the way and the truth and the life." Here's why.

Briana was irritated when she saw Austin following her to their table, wasn't she? In Briana's defense, Jessica had some strong words for Austin. She told Austin that in the future, if he wanted to speak with Briana, he had to come through her first. Now that's what best friends are for! Jessica is determined that no one is going to get to her best friend and upset her.

Jesus Christ had the same idea in mind when he said, "I am the way and the truth and the life."

Just as Jessica decided that she herself would become the only way Austin could get to Briana, Father God decided that his Son, Jesus Christ, is the only way God's daughters get to him.

Jesus answered, "I am the way and the truth and the life. No one comes to the Father except through me."

—*John 14:6*

Now, Jesus was a bold leader. He said many things that enraged religious leaders. This, however, is one of Jesus' most controversial statements. As you grow in your love for Jesus and the Father, other people will question whether it is true. That's why the next thing Jesus said is that he's the truth! Faithgirl, remember this: following Jesus Christ is the only way you can get to Father God.

If you think about the bond between Briana and Jessica, you can understand why. Do you remember how old Briana and Jess were when they first met? Seven, right! They've shared tons of memories and have grown to love each other deeply. That's how Father God and Jesus Christ are too. The love they share is extraordinary! Like Briana and Jess, they refuse to stand by and watch other people displease their loved one. God loves you no matter what choices you make. Yet, it is still displeasing to him when you are disagreeable and ignore his directions.

Jesus is incapable of ignoring Father God. He loves the Father too much to disregard his ways and hurt God's heart. Consequently, Jesus Christ is the only person who always pleases Father God because he heeds Father God's words without fail. Knowing you—both how much you crave Father God's love and how you can sometimes displease him, Jesus is the awesome big brother who steps in to help you. He simply tells you, "follow me."

Daughter Deed

To help you think the same way Father God does, will you do a daughter deed and focus on your BFF for a few moments? How long have you known him or her? Where did you meet? What would you do if you knew someone was irritating or displeasing your BFF? When you finish, take a few more minutes and write your friend a note of thanks for his or her friendship. Remember to drop it in the mail!

Thanks, Faithgirl! One of the ways you know God loves you is that he gives you good friends!

Do you remember what happened next, when Briana got mad and raised her voice at Austin? Their teacher, Mrs. Gray, approached the table and tried to get the truth. Initially, Austin denied that he'd called Briana "Butterfingers." Briana told Mrs. Gray that Austin was giving a false impression of the way things were.

Unlike Austin's version of the story, the truth is information that accurately expresses the way a matter or situation actually is. When you tell the truth, it means you're sharing knowledge as it is in reality. The truth is different from your opinion, thoughts, or speculation about the way things are. It is permanent, unchanging, and double-checked over time. For example, in Briana's case, she does not really have fingers made of butter. She never has. She never will. Nothing (including the number of times Austin counts her dropping the basketball!) will ever change that. It is the truth and points to what's really going on.

Jesus Christ described himself as the truth because he's what's really going on! Have you ever heard grown-ups say "It's not about you"? Sure seems like it's all about them, right? That is untrue. According to Father God, it's actually all about Jesus Christ. Everything you know as real in life is pointing to him. This is why he could declare he is the truth.

You see, God's plan is that the world you experience with your five senses—what you see, hear, taste, touch, and smell—serves as a foundation to help you comprehend the true, spiritual reality as you grow up. Your physical life comes first to prepare you for the new spiritual life you can experience in Jesus Christ.

You see, the world as you know it is temporary. Things around you are unpredictable and constantly changing. Jesus Christ remains the same. Remember, one of the qualities of the truth is that it never changes.

Jesus Christ is the same yesterday and today and forever.

— Hebrews 13:8

Another quality of the truth is that other people validate it. Austin confessed, and in the end Mrs. Gray orchestrated the extension of justice, requiring Austin to make amends for dishonoring Briana.

Austin's confession did more than enable Mrs. Gray to make a fair decision. When Austin finally told the truth, it relieved Briana. She was free to continue enjoying her lunch with her friends. That's because knowing the truth liberates you from the traps and pitfalls of life that try to get you down. When you're not tangled up or stuck in messy situations, you're free to live a joyful life!

That's why Jesus Christ followed up saying he is the truth by saying he is the life. Knowing God's Son, Jesus Christ, who is the truth, sets you free too! Free from what? you ask. From the temptations and tricks that try to slip you up and keep you from enjoying life. Following Jesus the truth gives you freedom from bondage, enabling you to walk joyfully into new life!

> Jesus said, "If you hold to my teaching, you are really my disciples. Then you will know the truth, and the truth will set you free."
>
> —John 8:31–32

Are you ready to walk? Then keep reading, Faithgirl; you're on your way!

Briana's Tidbit #7: I Am the Vine; You Are the Branches

Do you remember where most of the football team sat during lunch? Yep, you got it! Outside in the big open space called The Commons. They showed their team spirit and honor for the football players of the past by etching their names and player numbers into the tree trunk. It was a tradition that started when Live Oak first opened. To the team, that trunk was the vital connection that motivated them to win games on Friday night.

The trunk of a tree is like a vine on a plant. Just as the trunk of the Live Oak tree does, the vine provides stability for the branches of a plant, holding those branches up. Although the ground usually obscures the root of a plant, you can see the vine extending up through the earth. Vines also serve as a connector, supplying a pathway for the life-giving nutrients and water to flow to the branches. If you sever the branches from the vine for any reason, the branches soon wither and die.

Are you beginning to see why Jesus Christ said, "I am the vine; you are the branches"? He was sharing the reality that he is the strong, stable support you need to hold you up in life. It can get tough at school sometimes, right? Do you ever feel misunderstood by your family? What about boys like Austin Thomas who insist on annoying you? Sure you're strong, Faithgirl! But all of that is a bit much to bear. Instead of bearing those frustrations, trust that Jesus Christ is your true lifeline of support. With him, you'll exchange your frustrated life for one that is filled with good fruit—and makes Father God smile!

This is to my Father's glory, that you bear much fruit, showing yourselves to be my disciples.

—John 15:8

The vine is the extension of the unseen root showing up through the ground. In the same way, Jesus Christ is the extension of God whom you are unable to see. The unseen spirit of God provides life, like an obscured plant root. Nevertheless, it is Jesus Christ, the true vine, who extends that life to you, one of the branches. He is the one through whom all the blessing and riches of God flow.

And my God will meet all your needs according to the riches of his glory in Christ Jesus.

—Philippians 4:19

Aspire to make that flow through Jesus Christ uninterrupted. By saying he is the vine and you are a branch, Jesus stressed the need for you to stay connected to him. Branches are cut off vines for many reasons. Environmental issues like wind and cold, hungry wild animals, and bugs and insects worming their way through all pose threats to branches on a vine. You too face cold situations sometimes. Your circumstances might make you feel like a wild beast is trying to eat you up! Little by little, worries seem to sneak into your heart, like a pesky inchworm. These all threaten to cut you off from Jesus Christ, the vine.

One of the ways branches are protected is by covering or wrapping them. You can cover yourself too! Ban these branch cutters from your life with a covering of prayer, Faithgirl. Continue talking with God each day. Spend time sharing your thoughts with him and listening for his voice to speak to you. You may feel drawn away from God by many different things and situations. Yet to remain attached to Jesus Christ is to remain in the love of Father God. And his love is what you want, right?

Then, look to Jesus Christ because that is where the Father's love is located. Remember, in Father God's heart, Jesus Christ is the name and character who is far above everything and anyone else. Father God chose to invest all of his love in Jesus for one reason. Although Jesus is one with Father God, he diminished himself to the status of an ordinary, common person. Because Jesus willingly humbled himself in this way, Father God designated the character of this unique Son as the highest aspiration of all other sons and daughters.

Faithgirl, your beginning into the love of Father God starts with the humility of Jesus Christ. Humility is making yourself—your ways, your thoughts, what feels right to you—lower than God's ways and thoughts. You acknowledge that you can do nothing by yourself and become entirely dependent on God. And in that place of humility, you will find that Father God gives you the strength to love him back in the way that pleases him the most.

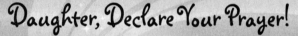

Daughter, Declare Your Prayer!

Father God, thank you for giving grace to the humble! Your special Son, Jesus Christ, is the way, the truth, and the life. May I follow him, my older brother, all the way to you. May I find your love in him and always stay connected. Thank you for choosing me and making me free to experience new life!

Briana's Banana-Nut Muffins Recipe

What You Need

1/3 cup applesauce

1/2 cup honey

1 teaspoon vanilla extract

2 eggs

3 medium bananas, mashed

1 3/4 cups whole wheat flour

2 teaspoon cinnamon

1 teaspoon nutmeg

1/2 teaspoon salt

1 teaspoon baking soda

1/4 cup hot water

Preheat oven to 350 degrees.

In a large bowl, beat oil and honey together with a wire whisk.

Add eggs, one at a time, and mix well after each addition.

Stir in mashed bananas and vanilla extract.

In another bowl, mix flour, salt, cinnamon, and nutmeg together, and add it to the wet ingredients.

Add baking soda to hot water and stir. Add to mixture.

Spread batter into a greased 9x5 inch loaf pan or into greased muffin tins.

Bake for 60 minutes for the loaf pan or 18 minutes for muffins.

Bread is done when browned and a toothpick inserted in the center comes out clean.

CHAPTER 3

Requesting Your Father's Presence

Briana looked forward to Saturday mornings. She was normally an early riser, but having one day a week just to snooze a little longer was nice. She was bothered when blaring music startled her from her sleep. Her sister's favorite song rang up the stairs, and Briana jumped up out of the bed, threw on her bathrobe, and marched down. Ashley was dancing and shaking carpet freshening powder on the living room floor.

"Excuse me!" Briana said, with her hands on her hips. "In case you didn't notice I'm trying to get some sleep around here."

"Oops. My bad. Sorry Bree. Got little people headed over for the day."

"What little people?"

"Madison and Mason."

"Why can't you go to their house like you usually do?"

"Their parents are doing some painting around the house, and they want to give it time to air out … and keep the twins from putting their cute little handprints all over the place."

"Makes sense. Well, next time you decide to do housework, can you please try to think about those of us who need a little rest?"

"What's wrong, kiddo? Did you do one backflip too many? I was hoping you'd be up to helping me out."

"No way, those rascals are twice as much work—"

"Fun … you mean fun. Twins are twice as much fun. I'll even give you a share of the money I make."

"Half?"

"Done."

"So, why are you so willing to share with me all of a sudden?"

Ashley shrugged her shoulders. "I need the help. I'm going to have to wash my hair for a dance at school tonight. While I'm doing that, you can keep an eye on the twins for me."

Briana gave her sister the thumbs up sign. "It's a deal. What time are they coming?"

"You still have your freedom for a couple more hours."

Briana went back up to her room and started getting ready for the arrival of the Foster twins. I can't wait until I'm a teenager, she thought. She had a list of all the things she was going to do in a couple of years. Her first priority was to take the babysitting class at the community center, just as Ashley had done. That way, she could earn money and save up for the musical horse carousel-figure she wanted to add to her collection of horse figurines. Ashley made a lot of money babysitting. Briana hoped to do the same.

By the time Mr. Foster rang the doorbell, Briana's focus on her money-saving plan had motivated her enough that she felt up to the challenge of helping Ashley care for energetic Madison and Mason. Boy, was she wrong! Ashley opened the door, and both of the three-year-olds were wailing as they flailed and kicked their poor father, demanding to return home with him.

"Maddie ... honey ... it's okay," Mr. Foster said. "Daddy will be back soon. Don't you want to play with Miss Ashley for a little bit while Mommy and Daddy paint your room?"

"No. Me go home with Daddy!" she said.

Mason jumped down from his father's arms, kicked Ashley in the shin, and then held on to his father's leg as if his life depended on it.

"Hey tough guy," Mr. Foster said, "that's not nice. Tell Miss Ashley you're sorry, okay?"

Mason started crying. "I don't want you to go, Daddy."

Ashley laughed. "Maybe I could help you more if I go paint!"

"Seems like it, huh?" said Mr. Foster. He looked at Madison, and then Mason, rubbing his head. "I'll tell you what, why don't we all go in the house together?"

They all came in, and it seemed like an hour to Briana before Mr. Foster was actually able to leave. He promised the twins he would come back and get them soon. He sang their favorite song. He offered to take them to their favorite candy store, if only they would stay with Ashley until he returned.

Finally, Ashley managed to distract the kids by pulling out some watercolors and letting them finger paint. It was a mess, but it worked ... for a little while.

Briana pointed to the objects in Madison's painting. "Who's that?"

Madison smiled. "Daddy!"

"Here's Daddy! Here's Daddy!" said Mason, pointing to the green blob on his painting.

"Good job!" Briana said. "Can I take these and put them over here to dry? We'll show Daddy as soon as he comes back."

The twins had forgotten their dad was gone. But Briana's words reminded them. She and Ashley looked at each other. "Way to go, Bree," Ashley said.

Madison started humming the nursery song "Frére Jacques" and crying.

"You want to sing, Maddie? I know that song," said Briana. "Are you sleeping ... are you sleeping—"

"No! Not that song!" said Madison.

"Then what song?" said Briana.

"Where is Daddy ... where is Daddy ... where is Daddy?" Madison sang repeatedly.

Ashley joined in, "He's right here ... he's right here," and pointed to Mr. Foster in the family photograph that was stashed in the diaper bag.

Ashley realized Madison was actually starting to sing herself to sleep. They all continued singing the song until finally, Madison and Mason were asleep in their high chairs. Briana ran and grabbed the fluffy red comforter from the linen closet upstairs. When she returned, Ashley had unrolled the futon mattress that the girls used for relaxing while they watched TV. Briana spread the comforter on top of the futon. They moved the Foster twins to the temporary bed for their nap.

Ashley held her pointer finger up to her mouth. "Do you think you'll be okay with them while I wash my hair?" she said.

Briana nodded her head up and down and pretended to swipe the sweat off her eyebrow. "Sure. I think I can handle it," said Briana. "After all that, I need a nap too!" As Ashley walked back up the stairs, Briana peeked over at the twins to make sure they were comfortable. That's when she noticed Madison's big brown eyes filled with water, and one single tear rolling down her chubby cheek. Too tired to put up a fight, the little girl just laid there, crying. Briana laid down on the futon beside her. "Madison, what's wrong?" she said.

Madison's bottom lip was perfectly pink and full. Briana thought if she stuck it out any farther, it would hit the floor. "I want Daddy. Go see Daddy ... pwease?" She looked at Briana, waiting for an answer to her tender request to go be with the father she loved more than anyone else in the world.

Briana's Box

Though Madison is only three years old, she does have Briana in a tough situation! Those big brown eyes were piercing Briana's heart. Now that Madison was no longer screaming, but instead softly pleading to be with her dad, Briana was turning to mush! With Ashley upstairs washing her hair, she knew she was supposed to be the mature, responsible one in the situation. Yet, she was confused about what to do.

If she went to get Ashley, she would prove that she was actually unable to handle it herself. If Briana called Mr. Foster, it would interrupt his painting project. If she did nothing, Madison would continue crying, saddened by her father's absence. As far as Briana could determine, she was stuck in a situation without a way to win.

She inched closer to Madison and stroked the little girl's hair. "Madison, I'm sorry you miss your daddy. I know how you feel," Briana said. Wait a minute, she thought to herself. Where did that come from? "I miss my daddy sometimes too."

Madison shook her head up and down.

"It's true," said Briana. "I wish my dad was here with me, just like you do."

"Where is him?" Madison said.

That's a good question, Briana thought. "He's away for a while. But, do you know what I do when I miss my daddy? I read stories that make me feel better. Can I read you a story?"

"No story. Daddy."

Briana could see that Madison was still exhausted. As she continued stroking Madison's hair and talking, it was becoming more difficult for Madison to stay awake. Her eyes kept rolling back in her head, and Briana knew it would be just a few minutes more and Madison would be back to sleep. Since not talking about Mr. Foster failed to appease Madison, Briana decided that if she listened to Madison talk about her dad long enough, the tired tot might fall back to sleep.

"Do you know your daddy's favorite song, Madison?" Briana said.

Madison smiled and shook her head. "Hmm hmm." She sang a tune that Briana was unable to recognize. "Daddy's favorite."

"Wow. That's a really pretty song," Briana said. "What about Daddy's favorite color? Do you know the color he likes most of all?"

Too close to drifting away to sleep, she pointed to the comforter Briana had spread over the futon.

"Red?" Briana said. "Is Daddy's favorite color red?"

Madison nodded one last time. "My daddy be back soon. Daddy said him be back soon." She closed her eyes, comforted only by the thought that her father would return to get her.

"That's right, Madison. Daddy will be back soon." Briana stared at Madison, thankful that she seemed to be at peace.

Believing with Briana

Have you ever spent time with small children like Briana did? If you have, then you know you can learn a lot by observing them. You can also learn about your relationship with Father God from the attitudes and behavior of small children. Sometimes big kids and grown-ups dishonor small children. Father God honors them above all.

On one occasion, people brought their children to Jesus, hoping that he would touch them. Some of Jesus' followers attempted to prevent the children from touching him. These followers completely dissed the little kids! Jesus was mad about it! He said to them,

> **"Let the little children come to me, and do not hinder them, for the kingdom of God belongs to such as these. Truly I tell you, anyone who will not receive the kingdom of God like a little child will never enter it." And he took the children in his arms, placed his hands on them and blessed them.**
>
> — *Mark 10:14–16*

Daughter Deed

Why do you think Father God values children so much? Can you do a daughter deed, and write what you know about the attitudes of small children? Think about Mason and Madison and their behavior when their father dropped them off at Briana's house. Why do you think they acted that way?

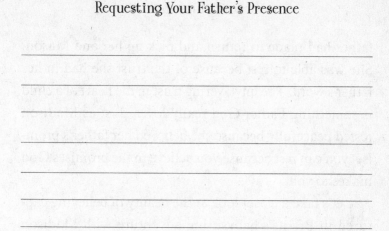

Briana's experience with Madison and Mason shows you how children feel about their father, and why God values what is in the heart of a small child. Remember when Mason kicked Briana's sister in the shin? Children, like the twins, love spending time with their father. They simply want to stay in his presence forever. Just as Mason and Madison kicked and screamed at the thought of Ashley and Briana taking them away from their father, children of Father God resist when people or the circumstances of life attempt to carry them away.

Father God also loves it when his children know what pleases him. Remember when Briana asked Madison about her father's favorite things? Just as Maddie was able to sing her father's favorite song and point out his favorite color, God loves it when his daughters focus on the things that please him.

What was the last thing Madison told Briana before she finally drifted off to sleep? Right! Our little sleepy-head was at peace when she remembered the promise her father had made to return and pick up her and Mason. She was able to rest because of the trust she had in her father's word. The unwavering trust in the heart of a child is something Father God really loves. Just as Madison rested peacefully because she believed her father's promise, you can rest because you believe in the promises God makes to you.

Let's take a closer look at the beauty of believing captured in Briana's babysitting adventure with Madison and Mason. Now that you've found Father God, the following tidbits will help you receive his love — and love him right back! Adoring Father God includes focusing on . . .

- The Father's Presence
- The Father's Pleasure
- The Father's Promise

Briana's Tidbit #1: The Father's Presence

Madison and Mason were adamant about staying with their father, right? Here's why. The twins know that being with their father is fun! Their father picks them up and puts them high on his shoulders where they can see everything. He sets the twins on his knee and bounces them up and down, like he's a horse galloping through an adventure in the woods. He lets them stand on his feet when he walks so they can take bigger steps. And when they are afraid of the dark at bedtime, Daddy comes and kisses them on the forehead, assuring them that he is there, and everything is going to be okay.

Father God's children know that being with him is fun, too! One of the best things about being with Father God is that he lifts you up higher. In the presence of God, you're like a small toddler on the shoulders of her father, seeing things the way he does. Maybe you didn't earn the grade you wanted on that test. Perhaps Mom won't let you watch that movie. Is there an Austin Thomas-type situation on your mind? You are not always able to see the good in every situation, but Father God can. When things try to take you to a low, sad place, remember to resist leaving your Father's presence! Ask your heavenly Father to pick you up and put you on his shoulders so you can see your life the way he does.

Being in Father God's presence is also like a small child bouncing on the knee of her father, as if riding a horse. As her father hums that old familiar, lively, and upbeat horse-riding melody, she closes her eyes and squeals with delight. Though the terrain beneath them is treacherous with bumps and pits, she trusts that she is safe in her father's arms. Likewise, the road of your life is complete with obstacles meant to slow you down or even wipe you out altogether. Yet focus on staying in the presence of Father God, Faithgirl! There in the Father's presence, potentially disastrous experiences become delightful days shared with the one who loves you most.

Praise Prompt

Psalm 16 helps daughters focus on Father God's presence. As you read it, think about all of the ways you benefit by staying with God. Thank him for the blessing of simply being with him!

Psalm 16

Keep me safe, my God,
for in you I take refuge.
I say to the Lord, "You are my Lord;
apart from you I have no good thing."
I say of the holy people who are in the land,
"They are the noble ones in whom is all my delight."
Those who run after other gods will suffer more and more.
I will not pour out libations of blood to such gods
or take up their names on my lips.
Lord, you alone are my portion and my cup;
you make my lot secure.
The boundary lines have fallen for me in pleasant places;
surely I have a delightful inheritance.
I will praise the Lord, who counsels me;
even at night my heart instructs me.
I keep my eyes always on the Lord.
With him at my right hand, I will not be shaken.
Therefore my heart is glad and my tongue rejoices;
my body also will rest secure,
because you will not abandon me to the realm of the dead,
nor will you let your faithful one see decay.
You make known to me the path of life;
you will fill me with joy in your presence,
with eternal pleasures at your right hand.

Madison loved standing on top of her father's feet while he walked. The steps that her father takes are much bigger than her three-year-old strides. His long, strong legs are able to travel farther distances much faster than she could ever hope to! Also, by standing on him and letting him do the work of walking, she can know beyond a doubt that she will get safely to her destination. Lastly, walking with her dad helps her understand how to walk on her own.

Father God loves this about little children! It shows that their hearts understand how to walk. He wants his daughters to love walking with him just as Madison enjoys walking with her father. Just as Madison's dad's legs are stronger and faster than hers are, Father God is stronger and faster than you are. By walking with him, you'll be able to go the distance in life, without quitting or giving up too soon. Also, walking with Father God is the only way to be sure you will arrive to the future he has planned for you, Faithgirl. Finally, walking with Father God initially will teach you how to stand up tall and walk on your own as his daughter. If you learn from Father God first ...

When you walk, your steps will not be hampered; when you run, you will not stumble. Hold on to instruction, do not let it go; guard it well, for it is your life.

— Proverbs 4:12–13

Nighttime can be a scary experience for toddlers like Madison and Mason. Admit it, Faithgirl. You even get frightened sometimes at night, don't you? What about after you watched that scary movie? Even though you know it's just a movie, sometimes the images that you've seen spook you just a touch. For small children, the knowledge of their father is assurance enough that everything is fine. They trust him to protect them from darkness and evil.

Father God longs for his daughters to demonstrate the same trust in him, even in times of growing darkness. Watching a movie is one thing. You can always remind yourself that a movie is not real, right? But, what about the reports of wars all around the world? Have you heard the true stories of young girls your age being kidnapped?

Those sad, dark realities could make you fearful. Instead of embracing fear, forbid it to enter your heart. If you feel afraid, act with strength and wisdom that comes from your Father. Use wisdom to stay out of dangerous situations in the first place. But if you do find yourself sensing trouble, shout for help, run to a well-lit place, do what you have to until you're safe. Discernment is a gift from God that helps us detect danger. It gives us an awareness to seek safety both physically and spiritually. Remember, you are a Faithgirl! What it means to be loved by Father God is that in his presence, you are safe from evil.

Daughter, You Decide

Do you know what to do if a stranger approaches you? What should you do if you were walking in the park and someone you did not know called you by name? What can you do to keep yourself safe?

Praise Prompt

Psalm 91 describes the safety experienced by daughters who learn to trust Father God and stay in his presence. As you read it, think about some of the dangerous situations you've heard about young girls like you being involved in recently. Consider some of the situations in your own life when you think God protected you. Thank Father God for keeping you safe!

Psalm 91

Whoever dwells in the shelter of the Most High
will rest in the shadow of the Almighty.
I will say of the Lord, "He is my refuge and my fortress,
my God, in whom I trust."
Surely he will save you
from the fowler's snare
and from the deadly pestilence.
He will cover you with his feathers,
and under his wings you will find refuge;
his faithfulness will be your shield and rampart.
You will not fear the terror of night,
nor the arrow that flies by day,
nor the pestilence that stalks in the darkness,
nor the plague that destroys at midday.
A thousand may fall at your side,
ten thousand at your right hand,
but it will not come near you.
You will only observe with your eyes
and see the punishment of the wicked.
If you say, "The Lord is my refuge,"
and you make the Most High your dwelling,

no harm will overtake you,
no disaster will come near your tent.
For he will command his angels concerning you
to guard you in all your ways;
they will lift you up in their hands,
so that you will not strike your foot against a stone.
You will tread on the lion and the cobra;
you will trample the great lion and the serpent.
"Because he loves me," says the Lord, "I will rescue him;
I will protect him, for he acknowledges my name.
He will call on me, and I will answer him;
I will be with him in trouble,
I will deliver him and honor him.
With long life I will satisfy him
and show him my salvation."

Briana's Tidbit #2: The Father's Pleasure

When you love someone, you know what pleases him or her. Not only do you know it, but you also want to be pleasing to him or her. That's why Madison started singing her father's favorite song when Briana asked her if she knew it. Madison knew the song true enough. Beyond that though, she enjoyed singing it because she knew it made her father happy.

Father God loves that small children know what is pleasing, and they want to do it. He desires that you too, as a daughter, will learn what pleases him, and that you will long to do it with all your heart as an expression of the love you have for him. Like Madison, Father God hopes that you will discover his favorite songs and sing them to him from your heart, even if nobody else understands!

He also wants you to learn his favorite colors. Yes, colors are special to Father God too! Didn't Madison tell Briana her dad's favorite color was red? Well, Father God likes red too, and he wants you to believe in the power of what the color red represents. Here's why.

When Father God sees red, it reminds him of his favorite Son, Jesus Christ. The color red makes Father God think about how willing Jesus was to give his life—his own blood—so that you and God's entire creation could be connected to the Father. Remember, God is fair and just. One of Father God's guidelines to keep things fair is that when you make an agreement with someone, you prove it by giving blood. Jesus Christ and Father God made an agreement in which Jesus chose to give his life, and Father God would forgive us and fill our hearts with love and devotion to him. Thanks to that red blood of Jesus Christ, Father God forgives you and draws you close to him as a daughter!

Briana's Tidbit #3: The Father's Promise

Since you're already thinking about promises sealed with blood, let's think back to what finally got little Miss Madison to drift off to sleep. Do you remember what she said to Briana as she closed her eyes? That's right!

Madison was at peace because she remembered her father said he was coming back to pick her up. In three years time, the toddler had enough experience with her father to know that the words she heard from him were always true. Even though she could not see him at that moment, Madison trusted her father enough to know that if he said it, he was going to do it. Rather than worrying about whether he was coming back, she took the rest that her tired little body so desperately needed.

More than anything else, it's that kind of heart attitude that pleases Father God. Children demonstrate this faith better than anyone else! If pleasing God is your goal, you will only be successful with faith like this. Here's why.

The faith Madison showed was based on who her father was. It wasn't that Madison believed it because it was a small or easy promise. She didn't only believe because he had picked her up from other places in the past. And, if anyone else had said those same words, she might not have believed them. Madison believed because she heard words from her daddy.

In the same way, Father God wants you to trust in him because you understand his character. As you grow in relationship with him, his desire is that you expect him to fulfill every promise he gives you because you understand the nature of your Father who made you the promise.

Among the things you have learned about God's character through his Son, Jesus Christ, focus on this as you think about walking with childlike faith. Father God cannot lie. Lying is inconsistent with God's nature. A person—like only God is—who is compassionate, gracious, slowly angered, fair, and full of love and loyalty for thousands of other people is incapable of lying.

The rest of us, though, are perfectly capable of lying, and unfortunately, we do. Often, we make commitments, vows, and promises to each other and we break them for many different reasons. With so many broken promises between you and other people, you could easily forget that God does not and cannot lie. Yet remember ...

God is not human, that he should lie, not a human being, that he should change his mind.

— Numbers 23:19

So, when it comes to the words of your heavenly Father, Faithgirl, remember Briana's adventures in babysitting Madison. Get the rest that you need from worrying about your situation. Father God's vows and promises to you are unchangeable!

Daughter, You Decide

Hate is a strong word, don't you think? It's hard to believe that Father God would ever use it, but there are some things he hates. One of the things God despises is a tongue that tells lies. Sometimes we lie because we think telling the truth might hurt someone else's feelings. Now that you know how Father God feels about lying, would you tell a fib to protect someone else's feelings?

Beginning with Briana

You, however, might feel yourself changing as you're reading all of this. That's a good thing! Maybe you're starting to realize you've let the business of school, practices, or church take you out of Father God's presence. Sometimes you can focus so much on pleasing yourself or other people that you forget all about pleasing him. Or maybe you want to believe in Father God's promises to you, but you have never even heard what those promises are!

Daughter Deed

If you feel like that might be you, can you do this daughter deed, Faithgirl? Grab a sheet of paper and some colored pencils, markers, or crayons if you have them. Write the words below on your paper, and decorate it however you like. Then hang it on your mirror in your room or in your bathroom. Every time you look in that mirror, say these words aloud with a smile, because they are Father God's greatest words to you!

> (Insert your name here), love the Lord your God with all your heart and with all your soul and with all your mind. This is the first and greatest commandment.

Got it posted up? Good job! Now, think about when you can spend some time alone with Father God each day. Can you wake up a little earlier before you start dressing for school? Do you have a few minutes after school? What about turning off the TV for thirty minutes and talking to Father God instead? On the lines below, write down when you think you can make time to share with him. What time and the length of time are between you and God, but do try to set a goal and stick with it every day!

_____

_____

_____

_____

_____

_____

As you make special time with him your number one priority, everything else—even pleasing him and receiving his promises—will fall into place!

 Daughter, Declare Your Prayer

Father, thank you for giving me a new heart and a new spirit. I will love you Lord, with all of my heart, soul, strength, and mind, just as you have said. It is my honor to make pursuing you my number one goal. I adore you, Father!

CHAPTER 4

Receiving Your Father's Children

The collective gasp of the crowd was the last thing Briana heard. After that, the pain in her leg was so intense she could only think one thing. Lord, please send someone to help me! With that simple prayer, Briana closed her eyes and drifted off to sleep.

When she woke up, she was a little confused at first. It didn't take long, though, for her to rub the icky crust caused by her dried up tears from her eyes. That's when she saw her right leg dangling from a leg brace, and understood why she was in Children's Hospital. Briana had broken her leg performing a cheerleading stunt at the half-time show of Friday night's football game. Not cool.

Jessica was the first one to notice Briana was awake. "Hey, Bree!" she said.

"Hey Jess. Please tell me I did not break my leg in front of the entire school at the game."

"Sorry. Don't besties always tell each other the truth? Everyone knows that it wasn't your fault, though. They think you're completely brave."

"Did Austin Thomas see it?"

"Yeah, but who saw you isn't important."

Briana's mom stood up from her chair and walked around to the side of the hospital bed opposite Jessica. "Not so fast, Jessica. Austin—and a lot of other folks—are deeply concerned about you. In fact," she said pointing to the door, "they are all just outside waiting to find out your condition."

Briana dropped her head and put her hands over her eyes, hiding her face. "Are you serious?" Briana said.

"Absolutely," she said. "They even decided to reschedule the game for a later date so your classmates and teachers could come be with you."

"So you mean I totally ruined the game? What a disaster! How can I go back to school now?"

A soft tap on the door interrupted Briana's frustrated inquiry. It was her pediatrician, Dr. Sutton. "Well hello, Briana, Mrs. Robinson," she said. "Looks like you have a nasty fracture there young lady!"

Briana's mom said, "Exactly how bad is it, Dr. Sutton?"

"Mom, chill," said Briana. "It's not that serious. The main thing is that the entire school saw me make a clumsy mistake and ruin a perfectly good football game."

"You know, Briana," Dr. Sutton said, "that's only one way of looking at things. The way I see it, what you call a clumsy mistake was actually a gutsy move that really kept one of your teammates from sustaining an injury much worse than yours."

"She's right, Bree," said Jessica. "Don't you remember at camp how we learned about spotting during a basket toss? If you would have let Isa hit the ground after throwing her up like that, she could've ended up paralyzed."

"That's correct," said Dr. Sutton. "Isa and her family have been right here with you since you got here, and I'll tell you what. They certainly don't think you made a clumsy mistake."

"We practiced that toss a million times. I don't understand what went wrong."

"And all of your practice paid off. You caught Isa exactly as you should have."

Briana's mom sighed. "Does she need surgery, Dr. Sutton?"

"I'm afraid so. The swelling is severe right now, so we're going to have to wait a few days at least. But I think surgery is our best option in her case. Take a look."

Dr. Sutton walked over to the X-ray viewer and put the pictures of Briana's leg to the light for everyone to see. Mrs. Robinson and Jessica gathered around as Dr. Sutton showed them the fracture in Briana's leg and explained why she needed surgery. When she was done, she walked back over to Briana and gave her a rub on the head.

"She'll still be able to cheer though, right?" said Jessica.

Dr. Sutton looked at Briana. "The rest of this year is out. You will have to go through physical therapy for a few months to get your leg strong again. But by summer camp, you should be good to go."

The thought of missing the rest of football season, not to mention all of the spring sports and activities, was devastating to Briana. What kind of captain sits out on the sidelines while her team does all of the hard work? She felt like she was disappointing everybody, including herself.

"You're a good friend to have around when a girl needs a little help. Is it okay with you if I go and share with your friends out there what's going on with your leg?"

"Sure. That's cool," she said.

"And how about visitors? I want to keep you in here this weekend and let the nurses help you get that pain under control. But you've got a lot of people out there who really want to see you now. Do you mind?"

Briana's mom answered. "Yes, Dr. Sutton, let's wait on the visitors—"

"No, Mom. It's fine. I'm okay, really."

"Are you sure, sweetheart? You really need to get some rest—"

"Seriously, Mom. I'm fine."

"Great," said Dr. Sutton. "I'll let your nurse know that it's okay for you to have visitors. Two or three at a time, okay?"

Briana nodded her head and attempted a small smile. "Thank you." Dr. Sutton walked out of the room, and Briana prepared for the onslaught of concerned Live Oak Lions headed her way. "How do I look?" she asked Jessica.

"A mess." Jessica grabbed a brush from Briana's hot pink duffle bag. She pulled Briana's hair up to a high ponytail on top of her head, finishing it off with a white bow. "There. That's better."

Briana tugged at the dingy hospital gown she was wearing. "And what about this?"

"Uh ... that stays on for now. You need to stay comfortable."

"Who says comfortable can't be cute? This is horrible! Can't I at least put a cute tee shirt on top before my friends come in? You did bring me something nicer than this to put on, right Mom?"

Mrs. Robinson shook her head yes. She had packed Briana's bag with everything she would need during her hospital stay. But it was too late for Bree to change clothes.

There was a soft tap on the door and Mrs. Thomas, Austin's mother, poked her head inside. "Knock, knock," she said. Briana's mom signaled that it was okay to enter, and the parents greeted each other. Then Austin's dad walked over to the bedside and gently patted Briana on her head.

"Good to see you, Miss Robinson. How are you feeling?"

"I'm okay, Pastor Thomas. Thank you for asking."

"Your doctor tells us you're in a lot of pain and will need surgery for your injury. I don't want to keep you from your rest for long, but can we pray with you?"

"I would really like that, sir."

Pastor Thomas directed his wife, Austin, Briana's mom, and Jessica to join him at the bedside. They made a semicircle around Briana and prayed for her full recovery. Briana had closed her eyes during the prayer. When she opened them, her eyes fell on Austin for the first time since he and his family had come into her room.

He was standing at the foot of the bed, looking a bit timid. She thought, he's probably just embarrassed by that big ketchup stain smeared over the number 23 of his Lions basketball jersey he's wearing. She pointed to the smear. "Did you miss your mouth?"

In the few months she had known him, he always had a quick joke. Not this time. He simply touched her on the foot of her uninjured leg and smiled.

"Are you comfortable?" he said.

"Not so much."

"That was a dumb question. I just want you to be—"

"I am." Briana reached to pull the blanket up closer to her waist, but she couldn't stretch far enough.

"Can I get that for you?" Austin said.

Briana was frustrated that she was incapable of helping herself. For the next several months, she was going to be limited. She didn't like the idea of relying on other people to do things that she was accustomed to doing on her own. How could she go from being the strongest athlete on the squad to a broken-legged bowhead in the bed? With tears in her eyes, she dropped her head, admitting to herself, her family, and her friends the frailty caused by her broken leg. "Yes, I need your help."

"You got it." He walked from the foot of the bed to the right side where his parents were standing. They moved back so he could adjust the blanket for Briana. "Oh wait! I have something else for you too," he said, walking over to the chair where he'd placed his backpack. He pulled out a white wicker basket wrapped in hot pink cellophane paper. It had a cute plastic megaphone attached to the top. "Here you go," he said. She had never seen a basket decorated like that before. Inside the basket were her favorite treats—mini banana-nut muffins and lots of fruit. "Just what the doctor ordered," he said.

"Thanks, two-three," Briana said. "That's really sweet."

Ashley walked in just in time to keep Briana from trying to come up with something to say to avoid the awkward silence. She rushed over to the bed. "Hey, sister. How's the leg?"

"It's been better," Briana said.

"I'm sorry it took me so long to get here. I had to wait for the Fosters to get home. With all those people out there, doesn't look like you needed me though!"

"Yeah. I know, right? Dr. Sutton said it was pretty crowded."

"That's an understatement, Bree. It's packed. I had a really hard time getting in here. Have you thought about going out there just to let everyone know how you're doing?" Ashley looked at their mom.

"I don't know about that. Do you even feel up to it, honey?" said Mrs. Robinson.

"Well, wheeling me out there would be much easier than trying to get everyone in here two or three at a time." Briana slicked her hair back with her hand. "Even though I look ridiculous."

"Sweetheart, you look just fine," said Austin's mom. She turned to Mrs. Robinson. "Maybe you should call a nurse in here to see if she can go out?"

Briana's mom pressed the call light beside Briana's bed, and her nurse soon came in. Mrs. Robinson explained that they thought it would make more sense for Briana to greet everyone in the waiting room and requested permission to take her out. Within minutes, Briana was up and sitting in a wheelchair, with Ashley behind her ready to roll her into the waiting room.

After Ashley mashed the button, the huge double doors leading into the waiting area opened slowly. Briana reached her arm back over her shoulder, grabbing for her big sister's hand steering the wheelchair.

"You okay with this?" said Ashley.

"Yep. Just a little nervous about all eyes being on me and my big blunder."

"They're not here to kick you because you're down, sister. They're here to help you stand back up," she said. Then Ashley pushed her sister on through.

When the doors finally opened, the spectacle before Briana astounded her. Looking at the cheery faces of dozens of well-wishers welcoming her, she felt like the bright lights from the football stadium had made their way into the hospital waiting room. The sight of the massive gath ering of friends, teachers, school officials, and church members flooded Briana's heart with gratitude. The painful misery of her injury evaporated among the black and gold balloon bouquets, the smell of yellow roses, and the sounds of her favorite cheer playlist streaming from the jam box. What mattered most, though, were her fellow squad members surrounding Isa who stood there uninjured, still in her Lions' cheerleading uniform, and holding a vividly decorated banner that read: Way to go Briana!

Briana's Box

Have you ever been to a hospital? You know it's one of the least fun places you can be, especially when you're the patient! Sicknesses, weakness, brokenness—like in Briana's case—are difficult conditions to endure. Here's why.

Do you remember how Briana felt when Austin had to help her with the blanket? Frustrated, right! She did not want people to think of her as a weak person who was unable to do simple things for herself. This is an attitude of self-reliance. To be self-reliant means that you believe you can do everything for yourself, without the help of anyone else. Girls who are self-reliant believe they have all the strength and power they need to get a job done by themselves.

Does this sound like anyone you know? The truth is, at one time or another, we all have demonstrated a self-reliant attitude! We dislike sickness, weakness, and brokenness because they force us to own up to the truth that we need help, destroying the wrong idea that as a human being you are enough all by yourself.

Father God actually goes against such proud, self-reliant people. On the other hand, do you remember what Briana finally said to Austin? That's right. She dropped her head and admitted she needed help. Faithgirl, when you bow your head and admit to Father God that you need his help, he gives you the special ability to accomplish everything he wants you to do. That powerful ability is grace, a treasured gift from Father God to his sons and daughters.

Like the coolest presents always do, Father God gives you the gift of grace in a unique package. Remember the gift basket Briana got from Austin? She had never seen anything like it before. The container was unique. Can you think of anything—or better yet, anyone—who is unique to Father God? That's right, you got it, girl! Jesus Christ.

Just as Briana's gift from Austin came in a unique package, God gives you his grace in his unique Son, Jesus Christ. Keep in mind that Father God pours everything that he is—love, goodness, compassion, fairness, and grace—into his Son, Jesus Christ. Jesus Christ, then, extends the grace of the Father to you.

Yet, not only to you! You are one daughter among many daughters and sons who are extended from Jesus Christ. Just like you, all God's children receive his grace. Grace works differently in each one. That is why it is important to accept your brothers and sisters. Father God has a plan, and every one of his children has a job to do to help finish the plan. The gift of grace is what God gives us to help each of us do our own part—a part that no one else can fulfill in quite the same way. Briana would not have received her favorite muffins, delivered with a joke and smile, if it were not for Austin!

Just as each of us has one body with many members, and these members do not all have the same function, so in Christ we, though many, form one body, and each member belongs to all the others. We have different gifts, according to the grace given us.

— Romans 12:4–6

Do you remember how Briana felt when she saw those doors to the waiting area open? Even though messing up in front of everyone at the half-time show bummed her out, Briana had an entire hospital waiting room full of people cheering her on toward recovery. You could say they are Briana's team, or family. In the same way, as a beautiful daughter of Father God, you have an entire family cheering you on through the game of life as you experience ups and downs, wins and losses, blessings and tough breaks. As you see your family in God show up in your life, may you be grateful, just like Briana, knowing God has sent you help. Are you ready to learn more about your relationships with brothers and sisters in Father God's family? Then read on, Faithgirl!

Believing with Briana

Who connected Briana with her family in the waiting room by rolling her out in the wheelchair? Right, her older sibling, Ashley! Ashley was the firstborn child of their parents. You have an older sibling—the firstborn—who connects you with the family of God too. What's his name? Jesus, you got it!

Jesus Christ is like Briana's sister, Ashley, in another way too. Do you remember that Ashley was unable to be physically present with Briana? She wasn't at the hospital at first. Likewise, your big brother Jesus Christ is not present physically in this world. Jesus lived as a man until his thirties. With his death, Jesus finished the job Father God had sent him to do in the world. Father God then used his mighty power to bring Jesus back to life and seat Jesus Christ at his right-hand side on his throne in the heavenly realm.

Though Father God wanted Jesus to be with him in the heavenly place, he also desired the work of his Son, Jesus Christ, to continue, so he could have as many daughters and sons as possible. While he was alive in the world,

Jesus went through all the towns and villages, teaching in their synagogues, proclaiming the good news of the kingdom and healing every disease and sickness.

— Matthew 9:35

To keep the good deeds of Jesus going, Father God decided that all daughters and sons working together would serve as Jesus's new physical body in the world. By following Jesus, you become a part of this body of Christ, learning his ways and doing what he did.

Whatever Jesus did, he did with a special attitude in his heart. Jesus' way of doing things was with an attitude of loving self-sacrifice. That same way of doing things — in giving yourself away for someone else's good — is how you and your sisters and brothers in the body of Christ will live now.

Having a heart committed to loving self-sacrifice meant Jesus endured some heart-wrenching conditions. Yet, he endured them because of how much he loves God the Father and you. Jesus Christ's loving self-sacrifice caused him to suffer:

- Rejection
- Sickness
- Pain
- Piercing
- Crushing
- Discipline
- Wounding

That's probably not an example you're excited about following, right? You don't want to be connected to a body that has to go through that! Well, hold on just a minute, Faithgirl. It's not the end of Jesus' story! Remember, he *endured*! Yes, he experienced it, but he also beat it in the end! Jesus was confident and reliant on Father God's love for him. He knew that if he would commit to loving self-sacrifice, in the end he would have great joy being with the Father.

For the joy set before him he endured the cross, scorning its shame, and sat down at the right hand of the throne of God. Consider him who endured such opposition from sinners, so that you will not grow weary and lose heart.

—Hebrews 12:2–3

Praise Prompt

Psalm 30 describes that though tough times do come, good times are up ahead for daughters who stick with God! As you read it, think about the people you love most in your life. Consider the conditions you would endure so they could be well. Thank Father God that because you're his daughter, your joy exceeds sorrow!

Psalm 30

I will exalt you, Lord,
for you lifted me out of the depths
and did not let my enemies gloat over me.
Lord my God, I called to you for help,
and you healed me.
You, Lord, brought me up from the realm of the dead;
you spared me from going down to the pit.
Sing the praises of the Lord, you his faithful people;
praise his holy name.

For his anger lasts only a moment,
but his favor lasts a lifetime;
weeping may stay for the night,
but rejoicing comes in the morning.
When I felt secure, I said,
"I will never be shaken."
Lord, when you favored me,
you made my royal mountain stand firm;
but when you hid your face,
I was dismayed.
To you, Lord, I called;
to the Lord I cried for mercy:
"What is gained if I am silenced,
if I go down to the pit?
Will the dust praise you?
Will it proclaim your faithfulness?
Hear, Lord, and be merciful to me;
Lord, be my help."
You turned my wailing into dancing;
you removed my sackcloth and clothed me with joy,
that my heart may sing your praises and not be silent.
Lord my God, I will praise you forever.

Now that you know that Jesus' way of loving self-sacrifice is temporarily brutal yet blessed in the end, you're probably beginning to understand the importance of accepting your siblings in the family of God. You need the grace that God gave them, and they need the grace that God gave you! Jesus Christ himself connected with others to help him complete the work Father God assigned to him.

While he was in the world, Jesus had followers whom Father God chose to help Jesus fulfill his purpose. In the same way, your brothers and sisters in the family of God are people he chose to assist you in getting your job done. As God's beautiful daughter, you have inherited a huge family who is committed to your well-being and success. Father God looks to your brothers and sisters as coworkers with him who make sure you receive your:

- Practice
- Provision
- Prayer
- Produce
- Prize

Now that's some good news! Briana's tidbits will help you learn more about these five functions of your siblings in God's family, so keep reading, Faithgirl. And hello there, sister! Welcome to the family of faith!

Briana's Tidbit #1: Practice

Do you remember when Mrs. Robinson, Briana's mom, wanted her to get some rest instead of seeing visitors? Like Briana, you probably wish that your mom would worry a little less about you, and allow you to make your own decisions. You are definitely becoming more responsible for yourself. Still, you want to make good choices that help you become the girl Father God intends, right? Then you need training and practice!

Father God will train you by giving you special members in your new family who function just like parents do. They are your brothers and sisters, yes. Yet, because they've been walking close to God longer than you have, they can direct and guide you the way that a mother and father do. They will gently serve you in the way a parent serves his or her own children.

> **Instead, we were like young children among you. Just as a nursing mother cares for her children, so we cared for you. Because we loved you so much, we were delighted to share with you not only the gospel of God but our lives as well.**
>
> *— 1 Thessalonians 2:7–8*

At times, you might feel that they are nagging. After all, you're no baby! Yet, they are teaching and training you so you will be well prepared to carry out the role Father God has for you in his plan. Training is a major part of parenting.

> **My son, keep your father's commands and do not forsake your mother's teaching. Bind them always on your heart; fasten them around your neck. When you walk, they will guide you; when you sleep, they will watch over you; when you awake, they will speak to you. For this command is a lamp, this teaching is a light, and correction and instruction are the way to life.**
>
> *— Proverbs 6:20–23*

Daughter Deed

Do you get tired of grown-ups constantly telling you what to do? Can you do this daughter deed, Faithgirl? In the space below, write how you feel about all the things the adults you live with ask you to do. Think about how doing those things is going to help you in the future. Do your responsibilities in your home really matter? Or do you feel like doing the same thing over and over again is just a big waste of time?

_____

_____

_____

_____

_____

_____

_____

Through her accident, Briana learned that doing the same thing many times is good training. Do you remember when Dr. Sutton told her it was a good thing they had practiced that basket toss so many times? If Briana had not repeatedly practiced catching Isa, she would have dropped her on the floor. Not good. The accident would have been much worse than it was. Yet, because Briana had performed that same stunt many times, it was a habit. Catching Isa was her natural response, instead of letting her friend crash to the ground.

Faithgirl, without proper practice and training, your decisions and choices will leave you crashing down to the ground and your life spiraling out of Father God's loving control. You may think it useless repeating tasks and assignments that your older siblings in your faith family tell you to do. Does Bree's accident change your mind? Instead, remember that your family is actually helping you establish wise thoughts and ways that lead to life.

Most of all remember, they're doing it because they love you.

Briana's Tidbit #2: Provision

Do you remember when Briana was trying to get all cute before her visitors came in? Her mother had lovingly packed Briana's duffle bag, filling it with everything she would need while she was in the hospital. That's because loving you includes providing for you. It was important to Mrs. Robinson that Briana had the resources she needed.

Supplying what you need is one of Father God's top priorities too. He wants to meet all of your needs, both physical and spiritual. Often, your sisters and brothers in the body of Christ are his instruments for providing the resources you need. Sharing is one of the best benefits of belonging to the family of God.

Now the multitude of those who believed were of one heart and one soul; neither did anyone say

**that any of the things he possessed was his own,
but they had all things in common.**

—Acts 4:32 (NKJV)

And you thought it was just a reminder for two-year-olds! Think again, Faithgirl! God wants his family members to share with one another, so that none of his children goes without the necessities of life. Let's face it, there are some basic things, like food, clothing, and shelter, that we all need to survive in our physical world. Father God expects his daughters and sons to distribute those resources to all people who are in need of them, and especially to people who are siblings in his family.

Daughter, You Decide

With so many choices these days, it's probably tough knowing the difference between a genuine need and a desire. A need is something you must have in order to exist. A want, or desire, is something you'd like to have, yet is unnecessary for your survival. What matters most to you? What matters most to Father God?

Do you have a responsibility to secure the resources you need to survive? Of course you do! When you talk about what you want to become when you grow up, it shows that God is already giving you ideas about how you will become a productive, resourceful woman. Not much longer and you'll get to it, girl! As you keep walking with Father God, you will become a mature daughter, who he blesses with so many resources that you have enough for yourself and to share with others. Until then, trust Father God. Remember he has adopted you into the family that includes your big brother, Jesus Christ, and deposited all you will ever need in him.

Briana's Tidbit #3: Prayer

Speaking of big brothers, Briana learned that having a big brother around can come in handy. Do you remember when Austin's dad, Pastor Thomas, walked into Briana's hospital room? He had little to say and assured Briana that he intended to stay briefly. That's because he was most interested in praying for Briana's recovery. He asked Father God to provide the healing that Briana needed in her leg, so she could return to the work of leading her squad.

In God's family, one of the most significant things your sisters and brothers will do for you is pray. You have sisters and brothers whose number one priority is to pray for you. Like Pastor Thomas, these siblings understand that when you walk closely with God, your prayers are powerful and they work! Pastor Thomas wasted little time but got right down to the business of communicating with Father God. Your praying siblings know that lengthy words are unimpressive to the Father. He sees you at all times, and he knows what you need before you utter one word anyway! The brother who loves praying for you more than any other, Jesus Christ, said you should pray like this:

> "'Our Father in heaven, hallowed be your name, your kingdom come, your will be done, on earth as it is in heaven. Give us today our daily bread. And forgive us our debts, as we also have forgiven our debtors. And lead us not into temptation, but deliver us from the evil one.'"
>
> *— Matthew 6:9–13*

What else did Pastor Thomas do? Right! He directed everyone else in the room to encircle Briana and join in praying. Faithgirl, you can pray by yourself, and your heavenly Father will hear you and respond. He loves you just that much. But guess what? The force of praying sisters and brothers is greater. Father God's ultimate desire is for a family, a large community of children who love him. Though he starts with just one person, his hope is that the one will expand to include many, many more people. So when two or three of his kids get together to pray about things affecting the family, he gets excited! In fact, he's so thrilled that he uses all his power to do what they ask of him!

> "Again, truly I tell you that if two of you on earth agree about anything they ask for, it will be done for them by my Father in heaven. For where two or three gather in my name, there am I with them."
>
> *— Matthew 18:19–20*

Briana's Tidbit #4: Produce

Two-three was starting to become someone special to Briana. You do remember who that is, don't you? Yep, you got it, one Austin Thomas. Initially, she seemed to care little for Austin. But, through her unfortunate accident and hospitalization, she was learning that sometimes bad situations actually bring out the best of what is inside of you — and other people you thought you knew.

When Austin showed up in Briana's room, it taught her that she really didn't know him at all. It surprised her that he even cared whether she was all right. Yet, as she stared at him standing at the foot of her bed with that silly ketchup stain on his jersey, she realized Austin really was concerned about her. The compassion he showed her by bringing her a basket full of mini-muffins and fruit made her heart thaw from the frost that kept her from liking him.

Producing fruit is another thing brothers and sisters in the body of Christ help you do. Not the fruit that was in Briana's basket, though! The kind of fruit that comes from being God's daughter. It's called fruit of the Spirit. Fruit of the Spirit are the character traits God's presence in your life causes to grow inside of you and flow from your heart. You can most clearly see the fruit of the spirit in the way you relate to other people, especially during difficult times. That's why when Austin showed Briana compassion, she was able to treat him gently. Despite his stupid jokes and her tough exterior, he's a caring individual, and she's gentler.

Father God uses tough times like Briana's injury to highlight the areas in your heart that are unlike his. He also uses people who think and feel differently than you do to show you where there are weeds and rotten fruit instead of fruit of his spirit! Even during unpleasant circumstances with imperfect people (which all of us except for Jesus Christ are!) as his daughter, Father God is cultivating these nine qualities to flow from your heart to your brothers and sisters, and even those people who are not in the family of faith:

- Love
- Joy
- Peace
- Patience
- Kindness
- Goodness
- Faithfulness
- Gentleness
- Self-control

Got fruit? Fantastic, Faithgirl! Fruit of the Spirit is sweet indeed, but the prize of Father God is better! Read Briana's last tidbit to learn why!

Briana's Tidbit #5: Prize

Briana learned that having a big sister like Ashley around does come in handy. Do you remember when Briana grabbed her sister's hand before they went into the waiting room to see everyone? She was feeling uneasy about what was in front of her, looming on the other side of those intimidating double doors. Briana was embarrassed, thinking her accident a clumsy mistake. Ashley reassured Briana that no one was looking to belittle her, but that the waiting room was full of folks who were there to support her. Then Ashley pushed Briana through to the crowd—with all of their gifts and gratitude—on the other side.

Faithgirl, what it means to be Father God's beautiful daughter is that there's a reward for you too! You have an inheritance waiting for you in the heavenly realm where Father God is now. Like Ashley rolling Briana in the wheelchair toward the waiting room, you just need a change of perspective, some encouraging words, and a little push from a brother or sister to help you receive it.

Your new family helps you see things the way Father God sees them. Sometimes, especially when you're not feeling like your best, you can focus on all the wrong things. You may dwell on the pain or embarrassment you feel, instead of the goodness of God that is in every situation. In Briana's case, she considered herself a klutz, but she really saved Isa's life—truly, a phenomenal deed in God's eyes! Jessica and Dr. Sutton helped her see it that way. Because your brothers and sisters are also following Jesus Christ to the Father, they can help you see things as God does when your feelings are clouding your perspective.

Relying on your feelings is a surefire way to defeat. Seriously, Faithgirl! How many times a day do your feelings change? Exactly, too many to count! Sometimes you need some help silencing those negative, false thoughts about who you are. God can use your brothers and sisters to replace those wrong thoughts with his thoughts about you.

Father God gave you sisters and brothers in the body of Christ to speak encouraging words to you. While Briana's feelings caused her to mistakenly believe the visitors were judging her for taking a fall, Ashley shared the truth that they all wanted to see her stand up strong again.

Sometimes you might feel like you're the punch line of a cruel joke. Yet, in Father God's family, no one is laughing at you when you fall. Truth is, we all fall many times, Faithgirl! What distinguishes a daughter of God, though, is that she gets back up again and again, because she's got brothers and sisters telling her the truth.

So, get on up, girl! You're God's child, and with a little push from your siblings in the family of faith, you're on your way to get a marvelous prize. What was waiting on the other side of those doors? Gifts galore! Balloons, candy, flowers, fruit baskets! What more could Briana get? Much more. What mattered most was the love and grateful heart of another person, and the acknowledgement that Briana had done a great job.

Make no mistake about it; your heavenly reward is great when you're a daughter of God. But the greatest of them all is love. When in the heavenly place with Father God, on the other side of your disappointments, sickness, negative feelings, and hard circumstances of life, the part of your inheritance that means the most is the voice of Father God saying, "Well done, daughter!"

Beginning with Briana

Hopefully, you're finished trying to get things done with your own strength, and by yourself! Briana has given you many reasons to follow Jesus Christ and rely only on the grace of Father God instead. By now, you also know that as a part of the body of Jesus Christ, you have many brothers and sisters cheering you on to victory! So, what's next?

Start just like Briana did. Ask Father God to send you some help. Briana had suffered a humiliating tumble to the ground, but the ultimate result was good for her. Had she not hit the ground and broken her leg, she might not have cried out to God for help. That desperate cry for help from the Father set off a chain of encounters with Father God and the people in her life that blessed her in ways she could not have imagined. Here's why.

When you ask Father God to send someone to help you, he does. Father God loves us so much that everyone who asks gets what he or she asks! So when you ask Father God for someone to help you, that is exactly who you get—the person the Father has assigned to be a helper. That someone is his Holy Spirit.

As your advocate, the Holy Spirit starts teaching you and making things clear to you, especially the ways and thoughts of Jesus Christ. Gradually you begin seeing things differently, just as Briana did. In the end, you will find that by the power of his Holy Spirit teaching you, Father God is able to make changes in your heart that you never even dreamed about—like Briana being kind to a certain pesky newcomer to Live Oak Junior High!

Daughter, Declare Your Prayer

Father, thank you for my big brother, Jesus Christ! I am grateful for the love that you pour out on him and extend to me. Father, send me your help. I want to live by your grace. Teach me to rely only on you to accomplish my part in your plan. Please direct me to my sisters and brothers in your family. I'm excited about receiving them just as you received me!

CHAPTER 5

Resisting Your Father's Challenger

Briana stood there in disbelief. It took Jessica to remind her that everybody was scattering, and it was time to go.

"Let's go Briana," Jessica said. "The show's over."

"This isn't a show, Jess. Are we going to just stand by and let this happen? Doesn't this bother you at all? What if that was us in a few months?"

"That could never be us. No matter what happens, I will always be here for you."

Briana smiled and hugged her best friend. "I know you will. It just makes me sad to see them like this. And now, Taylor seems to be completely out of control. I can't do nothing while one of our team members is about to get hurt."

"What do you mean? I actually think Kaitlyn can take her, don't you? She's one of our strongest! Remember that time when we were working on the pyramid for the game against—"

"Jessica! This is no time to crack jokes. I think we really need to take this seriously."

Kaitlyn James and Taylor Dawson were the talk of the day. Everyone was anticipating Friday night after the eighth grade boys' football game. The two girls, once best friends, were set to fight. Kaitlyn had emerged from last spring's cheer tryouts victoriously, making the squad. Taylor did not.

Briana had heard of competition splitting up friendships before. Yet, she'd believed nothing could divide Kaitlyn and Taylor. The two had been inseparable their entire lives. That is until summer cheer camp. Kaitlyn connected with new friends from across the country, and she grew closer to girls right from Live Oak Junior High. Girls like Briana.

One day at practice after school, Briana noticed that Kaitlyn had less pep in her step than she typically did.

"Are you feeling okay, Kaitlyn?"

"Sort of. It's really cool that you're asking. I actually miss having someone to talk to on days like today."

"Well, you can talk to me if you want. I know I'm not Taylor, but—"

"No offense, Briana, but that's what I mean. I miss Taylor. She won't even talk to me now."

"Seriously?" Briana asked. Kaitlyn nodded her head. "Why not?"

Kaitlyn explained that when they'd returned home

from summer cheer camp, Taylor seemed critical about the stories Kaitlyn wanted to share. "It was like she had something bad to say about everything I tried to tell her," she said.

"Did you try listening?" said Briana. "It was probably hard on her trying to figure out what she was going to do without cheerleading."

"I really did, Briana. I asked her questions about what she had done while I was gone. I tried to make plans for us to spend time together. And I called her every single day, just like normal." Yet, nothing she'd done seemed to be enough to keep their friendship alive. Soon, their once rock-solid relationship became nothing more than a faded memory.

Briana's mind flashed back and forth between her conversation with Kaitlyn and the unfortunate incident occurring right before her eyes. Even knowing the girls' history, she felt they were without reason to fight. She thought, why didn't they fight to keep their friendship alive instead?

For weeks, she'd watched them casually greeting each other in the hallways when they passed each other. Silence followed that, and then Taylor's visible absence from the football games and pep rallies. Now finally, something more had brought the former friends to the point of wanting to actually exchange blows—well, at least one of them. Briana was there when Taylor issued the challenge after the morning pep rally.

"You know," Kaitlyn said, "you're jealous, Taylor.

You were never my true friend. Why couldn't you just be happy for me when I made it, even though you didn't?"

"Me? Jealous of you? I don't think so! If I'm not mistaken, you're the one going behind my back, sending notes to my real best friend about what a loser you think I am! You're so afraid you can't even say it to my face! What's the deal?"

The growing crowd waited for Kaitlyn to answer the question. Did she lack the courage to confront Taylor directly? During the pause, Briana prayed that somehow the scene would end. She hated seeing Kaitlyn and Taylor at odds, knowing that only a few months earlier they were the coolest pair of friends at Live Oak. Well, besides her and Jess.

Despite Briana's prayers, and spurred on by the antics of Austin Thomas, the argument kept heating up. Austin squeezed his way from the back of the crowd to the front, standing right next to Kaitlyn. He held his hand out like a talk show host, extending the microphone in front of Kaitlyn's mouth. "Yeah, so what's the deal?" Austin asked. "You too scared to tell it like it is to Taylor's face?" The crowd laughed, and Kaitlyn ended her silence.

"Anything I have ever needed to tell Taylor, I always have." Kaitlyn looked directly at her ex-bff. "And I always will. I'm not afraid of you."

"Then how do you explain this?" Taylor reached in the rhinestone studded back pocket of her jeans, pulling out a piece of folded notebook paper. She unfolded the paper, waving it in the air. Briana saw that cursive handwriting in neon pink ink filled the space between its light blue lines. Kaitlyn always signed everything in pink and used a heart shape to dot the I in her name.

Kaitlyn snatched the piece of paper from Taylor's hand and started reading the letter. "I don't know where you got this or who wrote it, but it wasn't me. I don't have time to waste writing notes about you, so go yell at someone else." Throwing Taylor's so-called evidence of Kaitlyn's betrayal up in the air, she turned her back and walked away. "This is stupid. I am so done."

Taylor yelled to make sure Kaitlyn would hear her. "How about after the game tonight? Will you have time then? Or will you still be too scared to own up to your words and face me then too? You are such a coward!"

Kaitlyn waved her hand, disregarding Taylor's insult. "Whatever, Taylor. It's like you're punishing me for something that isn't my fault," Kaitlyn said. "Don't you get it? I didn't write some stupid letter about you, and I'm not the one who cut you from the squad!"

"You never did know when to close that mouth of yours," said Taylor. "I know how to help you keep your mouth closed though. See you after the game."

The cheers of the crowd gathered around the girls was deafening to Briana. While most of the other kids seemed excited about the prospect of Kaitlyn and Taylor fighting, Briana was determined to keep the girls from battling it out. She thought, should I report Taylor for bullying? Maybe I can talk to Taylor myself. Who really wrote that stupid note? What can I do to help?

Daughter, You Decide

What do you think Briana can do to help? What would you do if you were in her situation? Do you think this is a case of bullying?

Okay, that's enough, Briana thought. She spoke up. "Taylor, maybe there's a better way—"

"Briana, this is none of your business. It's between me and Kaitlyn only."

"Kaitlyn is my business . . . and so are you, remember? I know you're hurting too, but this is not—"

"Oh, I'm just fine. But you're about to be in a world of pain too, just like Kaitlyn, if you don't back off, Briana. I'll see you tonight," she said, before taking a couple of steps away from Bree. Taylor paused and then faced her former friend. "Besides, why should you care . . . and what do you know anyway?"

Briana's Box

Wow! What in the world just happened! Have you ever been sandwiched in the middle of a bad situation between two people? No fun, right? Briana's goal was simply to be a good leader and friend by helping reconcile Taylor and Kaitlyn. Unfortunately, she encountered resistance as she became involved between the clashing of two warring Live Oak Lions!

By voting her cheer captain for the year, Briana's cheer peers had honored her with the role of leadership. To them, she exemplified the qualities of a strong leader. One of the primary characteristics of a good leader is her ability to encourage the team. A strong leader is one who builds up and motivates each member toward success. Here's why.

Briana has learned the power of one. After months of practicing cheer stunts and building pyramids, she has learned that if one of them is hurting, injured, or not doing well for any reason, the squad cannot build. On the other hand, if one of them is doing well and really excited about something, that joy spreads to the rest of the group! One person really can make a difference, for better or worse.

Did you know that you are a leader, just like Briana? When you become his daughter, Father God gives you a position of leadership. You may be leading your younger siblings in your family at home, the youth of the church, or a club at school. Whatever your leadership opportunity, Father God trusts you, by his grace and with love, to encourage and build up, not tear down, the people you lead.

Just as Briana learned, whether the family of God successfully builds and grows depends on the condition of each of the individual family members. When anyone of the family is hurting, ailing, or unable to do his or her part, the entire group suffers with that person. At the same time, when one of God's children is doing well and is happy, we're all happy! The attitude and condition of one person will ultimately affect the condition of the entire family.

Do you think Briana has a relationship to those people that she does not lead on the squad? You're right! She sure does. To those people, like Taylor Dawson, Briana is still a friend. Because Taylor failed to make the team, Briana was no longer Taylor's leader. Yet, she did attempt to help Taylor as a friend would, by trying to resolve her accusations against Kaitlyn without resorting to violence. Here's why.

Briana understood that Taylor's removal from the cheer squad hurt. More than that, Taylor also felt not being a part of the team would mean the loss of her best friend. That's enough to put any girl in a really bad mood! Briana realized that when it feels like you've been kicked to the sidelines of life, you can take the disappointment, anger, and frustration that you feel out on other people. Sometimes, even the people you actually love the most.

Father God trusts you with the people you do not lead as well, Faithgirl. Briana befriended Taylor, even though she wasn't a cheer family member. In the same way, God wants you to live friendly toward those people who are not a part of his family of faith. Like Briana did with Taylor, you can ask God to help you see beyond the way people are acting and try to understand how they feel. When you consider circumstances from someone else's perspective, and then take the action God gives you to solve his or her problem, it's called compassion. Compassion is a major attribute of Father God's character.

Praise be to the God and Father of our Lord Jesus Christ, the Father of compassion and the God of all comfort, who comforts us in all our troubles, so that we can comfort those in any trouble with the comfort we ourselves receive from God.

— 2 Corinthians 1:3

Initially, it might seem that your friendliness and compassion is unsuccessful. Do you remember how Taylor turned on Briana? It seemed like Taylor was uninterested in hearing what Briana had to say at all! Yet, Taylor paused to think about Briana's words. In that brief moment of thought, she questioned why Briana cared and what Briana knew.

When you care about hurting people like Taylor Dawson, and you take time to show it, those people want to know your reason for even caring. Curiosity about you, why you care, and what you know is good. Do you want to know why? You are your Father's daughter!

Being the much-loved daughter of Father God means caring about what he cares about. What Father God cares about most is hurting, broken people who are not following his Son, Jesus Christ, to him. They do not know him. When you become a compassionate friend to such people, and they start asking you questions, you have the chance to tell them that you care because Father

God cares. The truth that you know is that the Father loves them too!

> **And he has committed to us the message of reconciliation. We are therefore Christ's ambassadors, as though God were making his appeal through us. We implore you on Christ's behalf: Be reconciled to God.**
>
> — *2 Corinthians 5:19–20*

Daughter Deed

Bullying is serious business. Be sure to tell your parents, an adult counselor at school, or another grown-up you trust if you or someone you know is being bullied. Being a Faithgirl, you also understand that Father God makes the difference, even in a bad situation like bullying. Can you think of anyone you know who regularly bullies or picks fights with people? Have you ever thought about why she or he acts so mean? Spend a few minutes talking to Father God about that person. Ask him if he wants you to help him or her. Ask him how he wants you to do it. Then, will you do a daughter deed, and write that person a friendly letter? Include why you think they act that way. Tell them how much God loves them. Your letter is not for sharing with that person, it's between you and God. Each day, continue to pray for your friend. As Father God gives you grace, your chance will come to tell him or her why you care and what you know!

As you continue thinking about Briana's dilemma, you know that initially she was uninvolved in this whole mess! She was just passing through the last of the students lingering after the pep rally, happily mixing with the crowd, until Taylor and Kaitlyn's public dispute attracted Briana attention. Eventually though, Briana's loyalty to her relationship with Kaitlyn made it impossible for her to remain disengaged. Briana made a decision to defend the welfare and interests of the Live Oak Lion with whom she was connected — her fellow cheer mate, Kaitlyn. Here's why.

Briana knew that she and the squad have to stick together at all costs. As much as she understood how Taylor was feeling, she refused to start acting like her and adopting her unkind ways. Briana and Kaitlyn were a part of the same cheer family, and Briana had to prove her loyalty to the squad and its mission of spreading Live Oak Junior High spirit among the students.

God has a mission too, Faithgirl, and you have a role to play in its fulfillment! That mission involves conflict. As God's daughter, you are involved in a conflict that you didn't ask to be a part of too. Until now, you've pretty much just happily followed your family and friends along, being the best Faithgirl you know how to be! As God's daughter though, you'll soon recognize that you're just like Briana—right smack dab in the middle of a war zone asking yourself, Wow! What just happened?

What happened is that by the nature of your relationship with Father God and Jesus Christ, you inherited an enemy. Just as Briana engaged in the fight because she was Kaitlyn's cheer sister, you are now engaged in a battle because you are Jesus Christ's sister. Your big brother, Jesus Christ, also named the Lion of the Tribe of Judah, has an enemy, called Satan. Because he hates Jesus Christ, Satan goes after all Jesus's siblings—including you.

Be alert and of sober mind. Your enemy the devil prowls around like a roaring lion looking for someone to devour.

— *1 Peter 5:8*

Yes, Faithgirl, becoming a much-loved daughter of Father God also means becoming a well-equipped soldier in an intense spiritual fight. For our struggle is not against flesh and blood, but against the rulers, against the authorities, against the powers of this dark world, and against the spiritual forces of evil in the heavenly realms.

So, you say, but I'm not looking for a fight. Increase the peace! Not an option, girlfriend. The fight is looking for you because you belong to the Father. Just like Briana ultimately had to step up and prove her loyalty to the squad by standing up for Kaitlyn, you have to be loyal to the family of faith by standing up for Jesus Christ.

Are you ready to rumble? Well hold on; slow your roll, sister! Maybe you could use just a bit more information about the battle, don't you think? As you read on, you will learn that the spiritual battle you are fighting with your Father God is:

- Invisible
- Interdependent
- Internal
- Intense
- Inevitable

Believing with Briana

The battle between God and the Enemy is invisible. Remember, the beauty of believing and having faith in Father God is that there is more to life than what your eyes can see. The things that you can see are actually fading away. It's the things that you cannot see with your eyes that are real. This is true of the battle daughters of God face too. You are unable to see the forces of darkness and evil working against you, but you will certainly experience their negative effects in your life if you fail to resist them.

Guess you had better learn how to resist then, you think? Follow the example of your big brother. If there's anybody who knows how to defeat Satan, it's Jesus Christ. He's the one the Enemy really hates anyway, not you. As much as you will struggle against the Enemy, it won't be to the same degree as Jesus. He resisted to the point of pouring out blood! The wounding of Jesus Christ on the cross was a bloody sacrifice unlike any other. Yet, the cross wasn't the only place Jesus dropped his blood.

One other place where Jesus bled gives you a clue on the importance of remembering that you're fighting a hidden, invisible enemy who must be resisted in a hidden, unseen way. One dark night, Jesus went up to a mountain he visited often, called the Mount of Olives, where he enjoyed spending time talking with Father God.

In that special time and place of prayer to his Father, Jesus shared how much agony he was experiencing, knowing that his bloody death on the cross was the only way he could defeat Satan. He prayed that if there were another way, Father God would allow him to do it that way instead. But he also prayed that the Father do what he wanted to do, not what Jesus himself wanted.

Knowing that his Son wanted to please him and complete his plan, Father God responded by sending helping angels to give Jesus the strength to pray even harder. Jesus prayed so hard, in fact, that his sweat and blood mixed and poured from his face as he reached up with all of his heart for Father God.

There, on that high, hidden mountaintop with Father

God and only a few disciples, Jesus Christ fought his adversary with heartfelt, agonizing prayer. That's how you will fight this invisible war too—with perseverant, unseen prayer, in a secret place, with a handful of your sisters and brothers who are following Jesus Christ.

> **And pray in the Spirit on all occasions with all kinds of prayers and requests. With this in mind, be alert and always keep on praying for all the Lord's people.**
>
> — *Ephesians 6:18*

Your sisters and brothers in the body of Jesus Christ are a critical part of the battle, because the fight is an interdependent one. If you want to maintain the victory that your big brother, Jesus Christ, won for you with his blood, then you have to depend on other sisters and brothers who are fighting with you. Here's why.

> **Though one may be overpowered, two can defend themselves. A cord of three strands is not quickly broken.**
>
> — *Ecclesiastes 4:12*

It is much easier for the Enemy to defeat you if you try to stand alone. Yet, if you stay connected and fight with your siblings in the family of faith, you can defend each other. When Father God first created human beings, he determined it was important for us to have help. Remember this, Faithgirl, no matter what it looks like or how you feel, you're never alone in the family of faith! But the Enemy of Father God sure will try to get you thinking you are alone and in this thing by yourself.

In fact, Satan launches a full-scale assault on the way you think, making the battle an internal one. The place where you have to fight the good fight is in your mind. That's why Father God calls his enemy the Father of Lies—because he tries to fill your mind with wrong information. Your protection against the false words of the Enemy is knowing and believing the truth of what Father God is saying instead. Father God has spoken in the past, and he continues to speak to his sons and daughters today.

In the old days, God spoke to our ancestors through a special, limited group of people he chose to hear him and then tell the rest of his people what God said. They recorded their experiences with God in writing, and you have much to learn from reading what they wrote in the Bible.

These days, God speaks to you, and all of his children, through the life and words of his Son, Jesus Christ. God is willing to speak and share truth with anyone who is willing to follow Jesus Christ to him! You can study and focus on the words and teachings of Jesus Christ in the Bible too.

As you pray for him to do it, God's Spirit will animate Jesus's words in your heart. They will become more than just printed words on a page. There will instead be a spark within you. That light lets you know God has just spoken to you! The words Jesus has spoken are full of the

Spirit and life. It's that life and those words that help you overcome the Enemy.

Still, the fight to overcoming is a hard one! This battle is intense, filled with extraordinary challenges and obstacles. Father God uses the battles to make your faith as strong as it can be. Satan uses them to try to accomplish the vicious goal he has for the people God created. That wicked purpose is to steal, to kill, and to destroy the spiritual life with Father God that walking with Jesus Christ makes possible.

If you are not already following Jesus Christ, Satan's first objective is to steal your spiritual potential. With God-limited and temporary influence in the natural world and circumstances around you, the Enemy tries to keep you distracted from the reality of the spiritual world, and your need for Jesus Christ and Father God. Yet, when your heart begins to think about God and his ways, you're on your way to new life!

The Enemy knows that the best way to ensure you never follow Jesus to Father God is to prevent you from thinking about God in the first place. In the mind of such a person, it's as if God doesn't even exist! This lack of consideration of God is a spiritually dead path you want to avoid.

As a Faithgirl, you are not even trying to go there! Thankfully, you're already following the way to life, Jesus Christ! Still, be aware, sister! The Enemy still has two other tactics waiting for you. Since his attempts to steal your spiritual potential were unsuccessful, now he works to kill your promise of reaching your full potential in God.

The Enemy slaughters God's promises and your life with him when subtle, wrong beliefs gradually fill your mind. After much time passes, these little thoughts grow so strong that they hold you back from moving ahead with your big brother, Jesus Christ. In the end, it's just as if a murderer has snuffed out the life of goodness that Father God promised you.

Sometimes attempted assassins are unsuccessful, though. Observant, alert people on the lookout for illegal activity often thwart their plans. You, Faithgirl, can be one of those people for Father God! When you are, there's only one thing left for the Enemy to do. When he's failed to steal from or execute you, Satan tries to destroy the abundant life that's yours when Jesus Christ is your escort.

What he could not steal or kill, the Enemy will lastly attempt to ruin. Faithgirl, what you don't know can hurt you. When you do not know what's on God's mind, the Enemy has a chance to sneak in and destroy the good work God is doing in your life. Father God knows everything about everything! If you learn what God knows, you can stop the Enemy from destroying your spiritual life!

Just as you do with any other person, you learn what God knows by asking him. As you invest your time in growing the relationship through prayer and quiet times alone with him, he sees that he can trust you. God wants to share information about his plans with his children.

"This is what the Lord says, he who made the
earth, the Lord who formed it and established
it — the Lord is his name: 'Call to me and I will
answer you and tell you great and unsearchable
things you do not know.'"

— Jeremiah 33:2–3

Know this, Faithgirl. Satan is cunning and covert,
deliberately cloaking his activity in darkness, masking
his evil as good. Yet, it's not his plans that are at work;
it is what Father God has put in motion. On your own,
it's impossible for you to know what God is planning and
doing. But, you're not on your own anymore, are you?
You're sticking with Jesus Christ, and he's leading you all
the way to the Father. Because of your relationship with
your big brother, Jesus, you can know.

I no longer call you servants, because a servant
does not know his master's business. Instead, I have
called you friends, for everything that I learned
from my Father I have made known to you.

— John 15:15

Knowing what's on God's mind allows you to flip
the script on Satan and ruin the ideas and plans that he
makes in opposition to Jesus Christ.

For though we live in the world, we do not wage
war as the world does. The weapons we fight
with are not the weapons of the world. On the
contrary, they have divine power to demolish

strongholds. We demolish arguments and every pretension that sets itself up against the knowledge of God, and we take captive every thought to make it obedient to Christ.

— 2 Corinthians 10:3–5

If you're starting to feel a little intimidated, rest assured that allegiance to Jesus Christ is the result of all this fighting. In the end, Jesus Christ and other sons and daughters (yes, including you!) win! Yet, you still have to endure the heated process of standing and fighting, Faithgirl. You cannot avoid this war. As Father God's daughter, your participation in this struggle is inevitable. Here's why.

Father God is a fair Father. As he rules the world, he desires to pour out justice on his creation, treating all people alike. When Adam, the first human being God created, decided to do things differently than the way God had directed him, Adam experienced separation from God. Remember, paying more attention to the cares of life than to God leads to spiritual death. Every human being inherited Adam's tendency to live like God doesn't exist, disobey God's directions, and do things our own way instead of God's. So, one man's error made us all error-prone!

In the beginning when Father God made Adam, his nature was just like God's — no errors, slip-ups, mistakes, or thoughts of himself whatsoever. But the Enemy caused Adam's character to change.

A different man decided he wanted to correct Adam's error and get him back to the original condition in which God made him. Do you have an idea about who that man might be? You got it! The man who wanted to fix Adam's error was Jesus Christ. He loves us so much that he endured the punishment for Adam's failure that God required in his love for fairness.

Father God looked at the situation with fairness in his heart and mind. If the actions of one man caused the problem in the first place, then one man's actions could also solve the problem in the end. That is God's justice. So, as a relative of Adam, you took on his nature. Bummer, right? Well, here's the good news! In all his fairness, Father God promises that when you're a daughter following Jesus Christ to him, you take on Jesus' nature, and become newly made in the way Father God originally intended.

Therefore, if anyone is in Christ, the new creation has come: The old has gone, the new is here!

— 2 Corinthians 5:17

And Jesus' nature is something fierce, Faithgirl! The firstborn Son of God is a warrior. Father God has declared that his Son, Jesus Christ, is the King of Kings! All great kings know what it takes to fight and win war. Jesus Christ knows this far better than anyone else does.

Who is this King of glory? The Lord strong and mighty, the Lord mighty in battle.

— Psalm 24:8

Praise Prompt

Psalm 18 describes how God helps his daughters fight! Read it in
its entirety if you can, and pay close attention to the verses below.
As you read it, think about learning how to win your struggles and
challenges in life just like Jesus Christ did. Thank Father God that
he teaches you how to fight like a Faithgirl and win!

Psalm 18:29–49

With your help I can advance against a troop;
with my God I can scale a wall.
As for God, his way is perfect:
The Lord's word is flawless;
he shields all who take refuge in him.
For who is God besides the Lord?
And who is the Rock except our God?
It is God who arms me with strength
and keeps my way secure.
He makes my feet like the feet of a deer;
he causes me to stand on the heights.
He trains my hands for battle;
my arms can bend a bow of bronze.
You make your saving help my shield,
and your right hand sustains me;
your help has made me great.
You provide a broad path for my feet,
so that my ankles do not give way.
I pursued my enemies and overtook them;
I did not turn back till they were destroyed.
I crushed them so that they could not rise;
they fell beneath my feet.
You armed me with strength for battle;

you humbled my adversaries before me.
You made my enemies turn their backs in flight,
and I destroyed my foes.
They cried for help, but there was no one to save them—
to the Lord, but he did not answer.
I beat them as fine as windblown dust;
I trampled them like mud in the streets.
You have delivered me from the attacks of the people;
you have made me the head of nations.
People I did not know now serve me,
foreigners cower before me;
as soon as they hear of me, they obey me.
They all lose heart;
they come trembling from their strongholds.
The Lord lives! Praise be to my Rock!
Exalted be God my Savior!
He is the God who avenges me,
who subdues nations under me,
who saves me from my enemies.
You exalted me above my foes;
from a violent man you rescued me.
Therefore I will praise you, Lord, among the nations;
I will sing the praises of your name.

Are you still feeling up to the fight? Good! Father God
has given you everything you need to keep from losing.
Come on now, Faithgirl! You know your daddy would
never send you out to fight unless he knew your foe's defeat
was a sure thing! Briana's tidbits show you the three principles you need to know to prevent the Enemy from stealing,
killing, and destroying you. You're going to need:

- Faith
- Hope
- Love

You Ready? Okay! F-I-G-H-T! Fight, let's fight!

Briana's Tidbit #1: Faith

Do you remember what the Enemy's first strategy is? Right, to steal the potential for spiritual life by keeping your mind distracted from the existence of God. Remember, the world that we perceive with our five senses is like a shadow. It's not the real thing, but it suggests the real thing. Satan tries to keep your mind on the shadow that you see in this world, so you won't pursue the reality in God. Yet, Satan is so *not* in control! In his love for you, Father God gives you faith to squash the Enemy's efforts to divert your attention from spiritual life with God.

Faith is an enormous gift from God. When you receive faith from God, he's investing your heart with the holding capacity to acknowledge that Jesus Christ is his Son. But, faith that comes from God includes more than room in your heart to acknowledge that Jesus is God's Son. Faith from God also bends your heart toward confidence in everything else that is true *because* Jesus is Father God's Son. When you believe that Jesus is the Son of God, and you are entirely reliant on Jesus for your welfare and the quality of life you experience, you are walking in the faith of God. This faith is what causes you to rise above the natural world around you and emerge as a spiritual person.

This is the victory that has overcome the world, even our faith. Who is it that overcomes the world? Only the one who believes that Jesus is the Son of God.

— 1 John 5:4–5

Would you like to know why the belief that Jesus is the Son of God is powerful enough to overcome evil? Because by identifying Jesus as a Son, Father God made clear that Jesus was a reflection of himself. Throughout his life, Jesus referred to himself using various designations. Other people identified him by an assortment of names too. Yet, when God introduced Jesus Christ to humanity, he wanted to show that to see and experience Jesus was to see and experience a representation of himself. So, he said, "This is my Son, whom I love; with him I am well pleased" (Matthew 3:17).

Hopefully, your heart is feeling that spark, illuminating for you why it is so important to understand what it means to be God's beautiful daughter. The Father called Jesus "Son" because Jesus represented God to the world. Father God calls you "daughter" because as you follow Jesus Christ, you become a mirror image of him too.

In love he predestined us for adoption to sonship through Jesus Christ, in accordance with his pleasure and will — to the praise of his glorious grace, which he has freely given us in the One he loves.

— Ephesians 1:4–6

Above everything else, the Enemy wants to wipe out the conditions of daughterhood and sonship. After Father God announced that Jesus was his Son, Satan immediately challenged Jesus' sonship. He continues to dispute the relationships of daughters and sons to Father God today. Yet, when you receive God's faith, and believe and rely on the fact that Jesus is God's Son, you defeat the Enemy's plot to rob you. Instead, you receive an entire package of good benefits from the Father who loves Jesus and you!

Over time, Father God by his Spirit gently guides you through lifelong discovery and exploration of the riches you will inherit as his daughter and fellow beneficiary with Jesus. With faith from God, you have a deep treasure chest of everything you will ever need to conquer every obstacle the Enemy sets before you because you follow his Son. And Father God gave the Son all his own power and the permission to overthrow Satan once and for all!

So, by all means, receive the faith, girl!

Briana's Tidbit #2: Hope

Overcoming the thief means Father God turned your mind toward him and gave you the faith to prevent Satan from stealing your potential for a rich spiritual life. That is fantastic! The Enemy's no quitter, though. He may back off for a while, but he will return when he thinks he has a better chance of taking you down

When he returns, he does it vigorously. This time, he'll be aiming to extinguish the spiritual life that you do have. He does it by targeting your mind with wrong beliefs about your future with God. Initially, these faulty expectations ignite your imagination, infusing you with excitement and anticipation about what is ahead. Eventually though, they burn your heart to a crisp, leaving you disappointed and wondering why a father who loves you would do something like that to you.

Dear sister, the Father who loves you is innocent of creating such disappointment. It is the Father of Lies who derails daughters from the destined future God has in mind. Rather than allowing the Enemy's false expectations to misdirect you, God gives you what you need to smother every faulty flame launched at your mind. Hope is what halts the Enemy's hurling of erroneous expectations.

Hope is confident expectation about what is going to happen in your future. With hope, you sincerely believe that something you're waiting for is going to occur in your life, although you have yet to see it. Think of it like this. Has one of your parents ever promised you something? When it did not happen immediately, what did you do? You kept asking them "When?" Right! After you kept begging (and they told you to stop whining, right?), you finally experienced exactly what they promised. That is hope.

Father God makes promises to you too. Remember, when Father God invited you to come and receive his gift of faith, it was an enormous package filled with promises. One of those promises is a hope, one single accomplishment you can eagerly anticipate is going occur in the future.

> **There is one body and one Spirit, just as you were**
> **called to one hope when you were called; one**
> **Lord, one faith, one baptism; one God and Father**
> **of all, who is over all and through all and in all.**
>
> *— Ephesians 4:4–6*

That one hope that God gives to daughters and sons along with faith is this: because Jesus Christ lives in you, you can expect that in the future when Father God displays his firstborn Son, Jesus Christ, to the entire world as the outstanding, excellent, and supreme ruler who God honors above all, God will honor you too. Sounds like an appointment worth keeping, right?

Then stay on track, Faithgirl, and avoid the disappointing false expectations of the Enemy. Embrace the one true hope that comes from Father God.

Briana's Tidbit #3: Love

When you've smoldered the attempts of the Enemy to snuff out your spiritual life, it's because you held on to the hope that comes from Father God. Way to protect your mind from false expectations! The Enemy still has one trick up his sleeve, though. Some tricksters just don't know when to stop!

Satan will stop at nothing to see you ruined. With this final tactic, his goal is to tear down the spiritual life that God has built in you. Hatred is what Satan feels for the Father and for Jesus, the Son. If the world around you seems to mistreat you because you are walking with Jesus, it is the Enemy reminding you that he hates your Father and brother. But, your brother said to keep this in mind about hatred:

"If the world hates you, you know that it hated Me before it hated you. If you were of the world, the world would love its own. Yet because you are not of the world, but I chose you out of the world, therefore the world hates you."

—John 15:18–19 (NKJV)

Jesus's words also tell you how to respond to and overcome the Enemy's painful reminders of his hatred for God. Do you want to know how a true daughter of the heavenly Father responds to hatred and persecution? She loves her enemies, she prays for those her mistreat her, and she does good even to people who hate her.

Love is graphic.

Love is patient. You wait until that person understands how much God loves you.

Love is kind. You are good to others because Father God is good to you.

It does not envy. You are grateful for how God has blessed you.

It does not boast. You accomplish nothing without God's help.

It is not proud. You rely on God for the strength that you need.

It does not dishonor others. You cherish all people God created.

It is not self-seeking. You give what God gave you to others.

It is not easily angered. You are peaceful because God's in control.

It keeps no record of wrongs. You forgive because you need God to forgive you.

Love does not delight in evil but rejoices with the truth. You are happy because God makes hearts free.

It always protects, always trusts, always hopes, always perseveres. You will fight to the finish for the faith!

Faithgirl, love never fails.

Beginning with Briana

In the past, maybe you've failed to see your journey of faith as a fight. Is Briana's experience with Kaitlyn and Taylor's scuffle making you think about God differently? Hopefully, you understand that there will be times of uncomfortable struggle in your life, yet God only uses those times to bring you closer to him.

If you want to fight like a Faithgirl right now, the first step is to enlist for combat. Remember, it's faith, hope, and love that defeat evil schemes to steal, kill, and destroy. Start by asking Father God to fill your heart with faith in his Son, Jesus Christ, and watch out! You're on your way to V-I-C-T-O-R-Y!

Daughter, Declare Your Prayer

Father, thank you for helping me trust in your Son, Jesus Christ! I want to fight with all the might you give me for the truth that Jesus Christ is the Son of God. When the battle gets tough and the Enemy attacks my mind, make my thoughts turn to your faith, hope, and love. Love never fails!

CHAPTER 6

Reflecting Your Father's Image

As they pulled up to their driveway of her home, Briana wondered why the porch light was off, and none of the house lights seemed to be on. Her mom always left at least one light on whenever they planned to arrive home after nightfall. "Did you forget to leave a light on, Mom?" she asked.

Her mother turned off the car. "I sure did. I guess we were in such a hurry when we left I just didn't even think about it. Anyway, Ashley should be in there. I can't imagine why she would just sit in the dark."

"She's probably watching a movie. You know, no lights give you the full movie theater effect."

She shook her head. "I guess so. Here. Take my keys. Go ahead and unlock the door for me, please. I'll start grabbing bags out of the back."

Briana walked up to the front door of her house and

struggled to get the keys in the door without any light. When she finally wiggled the key into the lock, she opened the door. She reached to turn on the entryway light and was shocked by what she heard and saw.

"SURPRISE!" her friends yelled.

"What are you guys doing here?" she said

Jessica, Ashley, and her closest friends from the cheer squad were standing in front of her with hot pink party hats on. The confetti and streamers they had thrown at her when she walked through the door lined the floor, and balloons floated across the ceiling, partially obstructing the banner that read: Happy 13th Birthday, Briana!

Her mother walked in behind her and then gave Briana a hug.

"Happy birthday, baby. I hope you enjoy your evening."

She squeezed her mom and then looked at Jessica. "I can't believe you guys got me like this! You totally lied to me! I thought we were going out tomorrow night!"

"Well, duh! They wouldn't call it a surprise party if you knew about it, right?"

Briana shook her pointer finger in Jessica's face. "That's alright. Just wait. Payback, my friend, payback!"

Jessica smiled. "I love you, girly. Happy birthday," she said, hugging Briana.

"Okay, okay. Attention, attention." Ashley jokingly cleared her throat. "Since our guest of honor has arrived, the party can officially begin." Briana stood beside her sister, holding her hand and beaming with excitement as she surveyed the twelve guests who had come to celebrate her birthday.

Ashley continued. "So here's how it's going to work. We're going to move from where we are now to the game room, which we have transformed for our special occasion tonight. We all know what a fashion diva Briana is, so if you don't have a flair for fashion, then this party is not for you!" The twelve girls screamed, giddy with excitement. "But if you are ready for this glam slam in honor of Bree's birthday, then let's hit the salon!"

"The what?" Briana asked, laughing.

Jessica grabbed Briana's hand and pulled her toward the upstairs game room. "Just come on! You'll see!" The rest of the pack followed them, and the blaring music Ashley turned on soon overpowered Jessica's words, forcing Briana to read her lips. "Are you ready?" Jessica mouthed.

"Ready!" Briana screamed.

Jessica pushed open the French doors to the game room.

Briana's jaw dropped in amazement. "Are you kidding me?"

The once plain game room was vibrantly decorated like a beauty salon! In the middle of the room was a lounging area with two swirl-shaped sofas and a glass table. The walls were lined with salon style hooded hair dryers. In two of the corners of the room were a huge round mirror, and a white table with all kinds of styling tools like hair spray, curling irons, and hairbrushes. One corner was decked out as a manicure station, and the other had a huge massaging chair with a foot spa at the base for performing pedicures. Sweet!

Briana's mom, Austin's mother, and their cheer coaches, Mrs. Hines and Mrs. Ward, were all dressed up like professional beauty stylists wearing fancy wigs, voluminous eyelashes, and white salon coats. Briana's mom had even thrown on a pair of crazy, colorful eyeglasses and a hot pink wig styled like a big beehive! She peeked over the top of her glasses and greeted the girls in a funny sounding French accent.

"Hello, ladies. Welcome to Salon Bree. We are happy to serve you today as you prepare for a night of fashionable fun." She looked at the other three grown-ups in the room. "Allow me to introduce my team."

Briana's mother introduced the women by their fake names for the night and explained that the girls would rotate through four stations in the salon — hair, makeup, nails, and feet. When they were runway ready, Bree's mom explained, they would choose a designer gown of their choice and walk the red carpet for a photo shoot. "So! Let the luxuriating begin!" she said with a wave of her hand.

Ashley got in on the fun too. She dressed up like a waitress in a café and served the girls chocolate-covered strawberries, sparkling fruit punch, dainty croissant sandwiches, and of course, Briana's favorite — banana-nut muffins! The older women treated them like royalty, styling their hair, and giving them relaxing facials, mani cures, and pedicures. As far as Briana was concerned, it was the best salon in town!

When the girls' treatments were finished, Briana's mom directed their attention to a couple of wardrobe racks in the corner of the room. Beautiful dresses of various styles and colors filled the racks.

"Now, ladies," she said, "you are to pick one designer original to wear when you walk the red carpet." She still attempted to speak with that crazy French accent.

"The what?" Briana joked.

"The runway. Downstairs. Now shush, my lady. Anyone who has undergone such a magnificent makeover will appear before the crowds on the red carpet."

"And what will we wear, madame?" said Briana, playing along.

"You are to pick one gown. My assistant Ashley will help you dress in the bathroom down the hall. Understand?"

The girls giggled at Mrs. Robinson and said yes before rushing to the clothes racks. Each of them picked the dress of their choice and prepared to walk like a superstar down the makeshift red carpet in the living room downstairs. Briana went first.

Praise Prompt

Psalm 104 is an amazing picture of God's beauty in nature. As you read the verses below, think about how awesome the Creator is. Then celebrate! The same God that made the world also made you! Now *that's* a good reason to smile!

Psalm 104:1–9

Praise the Lord, my soul.
Lord my God, you are very great;
you are clothed with splendor and majesty.
The Lord wraps himself in light as with a garment;
he stretches out the heavens like a tent
and lays the beams of his upper chambers on their waters.
He makes the clouds his chariot
and rides on the wings of the wind.
He makes winds his messengers,
flames of fire his servants.
He set the earth on its foundations;
it can never be moved.
You covered it with the watery depths as with a garment;
the waters stood above the mountains.
But at your rebuke the waters fled,
at the sound of your thunder they took to flight;
they flowed over the mountains,
they went down into the valleys,
to the place you assigned for them.
You set a boundary they cannot cross;
never again will they cover the earth.

When Briana reached the bottom of the stairs, she saw that the photographer was Mrs. Hines' husband. "Hey, Mr. Hines! You're a photographer?"

"I am tonight, Miss Robinson. Happy birthday. Now, strike a pose!"

All twelve girls took their turn walking the red carpet. In fact, they were so excited about their new image, they each took two turns, changing outfits in between. When all the walking, squealing, eating, and gift opening was done, everybody was exhausted! Briana walked the last guest, Austin's mom, to the door. "Good night, Mrs. Thomas. Thank you so much for coming and for all of your help."

"You're welcome, sweetheart. My pleasure. Oh! Before I forget." She rummaged through her purse and pulled out a cute pink gift bag. "From the Thomas family, with love."

Briana pulled out the glittery pink Bible from the bag. Her name was inscribed in silver cursive in the bottom right-hand corner. "I love it, Mrs. Thomas! Thank you!"

After closing the door behind Mrs. Thomas, she ran to the couch and sat down, nestling against her own mother who had finally plopped down. "How in the world did you do all of this?" Briana said.

Mrs. Robinson rubbed Briana on the head. "It's a long story. I'll have to tell you all about it . . . later."

"Watch the do, Mom, watch the hairdo. I just came from the most exquisite salon in town."

Her mom laughed. "Did you have fun?"

"You know it. I feel like a queen, Mom. Thanks for everything." She leaned over and kissed her mom on the cheek. "I'm off to get some sleep." Briana got up and headed up the stairs to her bedroom. Before she went to bed though, she wanted to take one last peek in the game room, to look at the place of the best birthday party she'd ever had. There was one final surprise waiting for her.

Austin Taylor was in the game room sweeping up the floor. Briana interrupted his whistling.

"Hey, Austin. I didn't know —"

"Yeah, we're just cleaning up."

"Who's we?"

"Me, my dad, and Mr. Hines. They're loading up some stuff in the truck."

"So, you mean you guys are the ones who did all of this for me? Have you been here all night?"

"Yep. Between me, my dad, and Mr. Hines, you're looking at your videographer, your set designer, your chef, your security guard, and —"

" ... and my photographer. I never even noticed you guys were here working so hard."

"Well, it was kind of a girly thing you know, not really the place for a bunch of guys, know what I mean?"

"I get it, Austin. It's hard for me to believe that you'd be willing to give up your Friday night for this." She grabbed a bottle of pink nail polish and shook it. "Your dad must have forced you to do it."

"No, not exactly. My dad is cool. We have fun hanging out together."

"So how long have you known about this?"

"I've been in on it since the beginning. It was actually Dad's bright idea, but he wanted to keep it a secret. I promised him I wouldn't do or say anything to tip you off."

"No way! Why would he do all of this for me? Wait a minute. Did my mom pay you guys or something? I can't do enough chores to pay you for this!"

Austin shrugged his shoulders and kept working, not noticing the disbelief on Briana's face. "Don't worry about paying for it, Bree. The cost is taken care of." He stopped cleaning long enough to look at Briana. He smiled, and she noticed that he was starting to blush. He quickly looked away. "You look st—"

Briana was afraid to know what Austin thought about her makeover. Was he going to say stupid? Or straight up ridiculous? It could be stunning, but she didn't give him the chance to finish. "So uh, you and your dad, I mean, you really get along well?"

"Yeah. He's got mad love because I'm his first son and the only one. That whole thing."

"Must be nice."

"Yes and no." He grabbed a bottle of water and took a sip. "Yes, because everything he gives, he gives to me. Not just stuff. You know what I mean? It's like, he loves the things . . . the people . . . that I love."

"And the no?"

"I know he wanted more kids. He wanted a huge family and never meant for me to be the only child. I think that's why he does so much for my friends. If you're connected to me, then he treats you the way he treats me. It's like you become a part of us. I don't know. He's just cool like that."

Pastor Taylor walked into the game room, interrupting their conversation. "Who's cool like what?" He didn't wait for an answer. "Wow, Briana! You look fabulous. Now that's what you call a makeover, huh? You're destined for stardom young lady." He grabbed a couple of chairs and walked back out to go load them in the truck.

"I agree," Austin said, "Oh! Hey, I've got something for you." He grabbed a DVD and a long white envelope off the table. "Here you go. The video of your party."

"Awesome! I guess now I can have another party to watch the party!" She held up the envelope, ignoring the handwriting on the front. "And what's this?"

"Nothing much. Just a little something I wanted to share with you."

She read the small, scrawny cursive on the envelope: To Briana, Love Austin.

Briana's Box

Say what! No, Austin Thomas did not just use the *L* word! Okay, maybe he didn't actually say he loved Briana, but still! Briana felt a little strange, and yes, excited even, about the way Austin was talking. Knowing that he cared made her feel special. It had taken her some time to warm up to Austin, but since they had become friends, her life did seem to be changing for the better.

Daughter, You Decide

It sure sounds like Briana and Austin are headed in a special direction, don't you think? Their parents are so *not* about to let them date at their age! But she's not even sure how she's supposed to feel about it. And she surely doesn't know how to respond to him. Daughter, you decide. What would you do if a boy gave you a letter like the one Austin gave Briana?

Briana realized that her own situation with her father might not ever change. She had grown accustomed to seeing other girls with their fathers. Yet seeing Austin with his dad was teaching her new things about the way fathers love their sons, especially the one who was born first! That's important for you to understand too. Here's why.

Briana's experience with Austin and his dad is similar to your experience with Father God and his first Son, Jesus Christ. Remember why Austin said his father loved him so much? Right! Austin was his father's first and only son. As the only son, Austin was the recipient of all of his father's love, gifts, and energy. But, Austin knew that his father wanted more children.

Likewise, in the beginning, Jesus Christ was the first and only Son of Father God. Because he had no other children yet, Father God poured all of his love, gifts, and energy into Jesus Christ. Yet, the Father's desire and intention was always to have a large family full of daughters and sons that he could love.

Do you remember what Austin's dad did to meet his desire to have more children to love? Yes! He loved Austin's friends. Whomever Austin loved and cared about, his father loved and cared for too. Austin's father welcomed his son's friends, like Briana, into their relationship because Austin loved them.

This is exactly what Father God does as well. To fulfill the desire in his heart for a large family full of daughters and sons, he loves whomever his first Son, Jesus Christ, loves. Whomever Jesus loves, the Father loves. He welcomes friends of Jesus Christ, like you, into the loving bond that the two of them share.

The way people see the bond of love between Austin and his dad is when they work together. Because of how much they love each other, Pastor Thomas and Austin enjoy collaborating. They coordinated every detail to pull off Briana's party according to the original plan. Lastly, Austin was careful to do only what his father instructed him to do and say. Briana was astonished that Austin was in on it from the start, and that he kept quiet about it the entire time!

Just like Austin and his dad, Father God and Jesus have been joyfully working together from the start. They make every detail of God's plan flow together so it ends exactly the way the Father originally intended. Just like Austin, Jesus followed Father God's directions with diligence, carrying out the plan to perfect completion.

When the girls completed their makeovers, they walked downstairs like superstars to parade down the red carpet and shine in front of the camera. Aside from having great fun in the process, the highlight and purpose of the entire evening was transformation into an image that, as Pastor Thomas said to Briana, made her destined for stardom.

Your future and destiny from Father God includes shining like a star too. You might not see your name in the bright lights of LA, or a star on the Hollywood walk-of-fame might not be in your future. Yet, the red carpets of this world that we see with our eyes are fading, and there is honor in your future from Father God, which lasts forever.

Even though the girls had a blast celebrating her birthday, the point of Briana's party was to transform each girl into an image worthy of honor. That, Faithgirl, is also the point of everything God is doing in your life. The desire of Father God's heart is to transform you into the image of the one person suitable to be exalted, like a shining star. Do you know who that person is? You guessed it, girl! That person is Jesus Christ.

Believing with Briana

Your makeover into the image of Jesus Christ is a special piece of God's ultimate work of art. You could think of yourself as one line in the perfect love poem! Father God reproducing the life of Jesus Christ in us is accomplished:

- Discreetly
- Divinely
- Definitely

Do you remember where the celebration honoring Briana's birthday started? Upstairs in the game room, right! The privacy behind those closed French doors was just right for transforming ordinary young women into extraordinary models of perfection. The girls needed much help with their makeovers. After all, skilled artists who know exactly how a model is supposed to look do the best makeovers. Her mother, cheer coaches, Mrs. Thomas, and Ashley all contributed to the process. Before receiving the honor of walking the red carpet, they underwent treatment at five stations: hairstyling, facial, manicure, pedicures, and wardrobe.

Walking through the process of transformation could be embarrassing, so Father God begins discreetly, too. Before you're ready for the public, Father God prepares you in private. If you've ever seen a makeover, you know this is the loving thing to do! Makeovers get messy and ugly before they get pretty. Father God is not out to shame you in front of everybody else. A beauty queen in the Bible, named Esther, had a fabulous (and long!) makeover in private too, before she went public.

> **Before a young woman's turn came to go in to King Xerxes, she had to complete twelve months of beauty treatments prescribed for the women, six months with oil of myrrh and six with perfumes and cosmetics.**
>
> *— Esther 2:12*

Esther had people helping her too, just as Briana did. Father God does not leave you helpless either. Your makeover is divinely inspired. The best person for the job of reproducing Jesus Christ in you is the Holy Spirit. The Holy Spirit knows exactly what Jesus looks like, and the Spirit is skilled at re-creating that same look in you. He does it by guiding you through various circumstances of life and training you in those situations.

Briana's makeover consisted of stops at five different stations before she was fit for public display. At each of those five stops, the stylist formed some feature of Briana in a new way. Each girl was given a new look in relation to her hair, the features on her face, her hands, her feet, and the clothes she wore.

Likewise, the Holy Spirit will guide you to specific experiences and newly form the characteristics of Jesus Christ in you. The Spirit restyles your hair, or what is growing out of your head. If you're going to shine for your heavenly Father, then your mind has to change.

Who has known the mind of the Lord so as to instruct him? But we have the mind of Christ.

— 1 Corinthians 2:16

You remember that your mind is where the battle is, don't you? So make sure you see your stylist, the Holy Spirit, to get the Jesus Christ cut!

Please keep it moving though, because there is more new styling on the way. The Holy Spirit will also attend to the features on your face. Your nose, eyes, ears, and mouth require major reconstruction to the pattern of Jesus Christ if you're going to light up the world with Father God!

Your nose, eyes, ears, and mouth let you know what's up in the natural world around you. That's exactly what they do in the spiritual world too. Your spiritual life is sensational! You don't think so? Well, think again, Faithgirl! The knowledge of Jesus Christ has a distinctive aroma, like a sweet-smelling fragrance you can detect with your nose. When the Holy Spirit makes over your eyes, you learn what it means to look good to Father God, the way Jesus does.

Do nothing out of selfish ambition or vain conceit. Rather, in humility value others above yourselves, not looking to your own interests but each of you to the interests of the others.
— *Philippians 2:3–4*

Ears are important too, because Jesus Christ made decisions based on what he heard Father God speak. And speaking of speaking! The matter of your mouth is urgent and powerful, dear sister, so the Holy Spirit must fill it with Christ's words of life.

The last two game room stations that Briana and the girls went to both involved large tubs filled with water. Don't you enjoy soaking your hands and feet in a bin of warm water all bubbly with soap? Briana's manicure left her hands feeling clean and rejuvenated. The pedicure, which was her last stop before wardrobe down the hall in the bathroom, made her feet feel brand new and ready to walk with some pep in her step!

Just as it was during Briana's makeover, warm water and cleansing are a major part of the Holy Spirit making room for the life of Jesus Christ to show up in you. Father God wants his children to worship him with uplifted hands that are clean, rather than unclean as if they've worshiped a false god. Jesus demonstrated what the touch of a daughter or son with clean, refreshed hands like his can do.

> **When Jesus came into Peter's house, he saw Peter's mother-in-law lying in bed with a fever. He touched her hand and the fever left her, and she got up and began to wait on him.**
>
> — *Matthew 8:14–15*

The Father looks for more than just clean hands though, so the Holy Spirit will also get your feet ready for you to walk out your life in the way that Jesus did. As the master artist who transforms you, the Spirit gives you the understanding and wisdom necessary to live a life that honors and pleases God in every way. The Holy Spirit uses the feet of Jesus as a mold for your own, setting you up to walk as he did. Here's how you get to stepping:

> **Follow God's example, therefore, as dearly loved children and walk in the way of love, just as Christ loved us and gave himself up for us as a fragrant offering and sacrifice to God.**
>
> — *Ephesians 5:1–2*

When it was time to get dressed in their beautiful gowns, Briana fell in love with the long white one embellished with beading and crystals. It was a good thing Ashley was there to assist her, because it would have been impossible for her to dress herself. She polished off her ensemble with simple, yet elegant jewelry and a classic pair of sateen ballet flats. The final adornment, which sealed her status as the center of attention, was a petite tiara that sat modestly on her beautifully styled head. Without a doubt, she definitely was flawless in her appearance.

A flawless appearance before him is what your heavenly Father has planned for you too. The model he uses to assess your completeness is the Son he loves so greatly, Jesus Christ. Briana was able to finish flawlessly with the help of Ashley, her assistant for the evening. Likewise, the Holy Spirit, your helper sent to you from Father God, will enable you to walk into your future as a daughter made over into the image of his Son, Jesus Christ. Before him you will stand in unsurpassed and flawless beauty.

There is no doubt about this, Faithgirl. This is the future and destiny of all daughters and sons of Father God. He definitely determined it before he even created the world! So, since it's a done deal, do you want to know exactly how you will look?

Then look no farther than your brother, Jesus Christ, and to Briana's tidbits that include three insights into Jesus' nature. Three statements Jesus made (yep, some more "I AM" thoughts) show what he is like, and what you are becoming by the work of the Holy Spirit. Jesus said,

- I AM Gentle
- I AM Humble in Heart
- I AM Generous

Just as Austin did for Briana, Jesus has left you a special letter telling you what he's like inside. Make sure you read it in a quiet place, when you have some time alone. Imagine that Jesus is sitting right there next to you, waiting for you to follow him to Father God.

Dear Faithgirl,

I am gentle. I know you've been hearing a lot about bullying lately, but I'm no bully. Other people may get rough or violent with you, trying to make you do things their way. Just as heaven is higher up than the earth, my ways are higher than yours are. Still, I will not use force to bring you near to me. I am kind and mild when I invite you to walk with me. My hope is that you will follow me because you love me, not because you are afraid of me. Sometimes you don't always recognize my voice because I am soft-spoken, but I'm constantly calling you. When I bring you to me, I do it with kindness. My kindness always works.

I am humble in heart too. I understand other people can make you feel nervous and afraid sometimes, with all of their rules and regulations: "Do this, don't do that." They act as if the entire world revolves around them. I am not like that. I'm very simple and don't claim to be so important and special that you can't approach me. When I see that life is weighing you down, it makes my heart heavy with sadness. So, I'll get down in the dirty, messy situations of life with you, no matter what other people think. After that, I'll make a swap with you.

I trade you because I am generous. I love to give. So, when I bend down to pick you up, you can give me the ashes of the mess in your life. Then, I will give you the crown of beautiful life spent walking with Father God. I understand you think you don't deserve it. Remember though, this life really isn't about you or what you think. It's all about Father God and what he thinks. He thinks that because I was willing to give my life, the most valuable thing that a person can give, you do deserve it. According to Father God, whomever I love and cherish deserves to receive good gifts. And guess what, daughter of God? I love you.

Daughter Deed

Jesus is always inviting you to spend time with him. He wants to take you to the heavenly Father in prayer. Now that you've read your letter from Jesus, will you do a daughter deed? Write a letter back to Jesus in the space below, telling him how you feel about his letter. Do you want the Holy Spirit to make you over into his image?

_____

_____

_____

_____

_____

_____

_____

_____

_____

_____

Beginning with Briana

In the natural world, salon visits and makeovers are great! Still, the spiritual beauty that radiates from within you matters most to Father God. Fancy clothes, blingy jewelry, and hair whipped just right are not the things that make you beautiful. In God's sight, a daughter's gentle and peaceful spirit shining outwardly is priceless and unfading.

Charm is deceptive, and beauty is fleeting; but a woman who fears the LORD is to be praised.

— *Proverbs 31:30*

 Daughter, Declare Your Prayer

Father, thank you for choosing to make me over! I am grateful for the work of your Holy Spirit within me. May I always be willing to learn from you. I'm excited about becoming a reflection of Jesus Christ, the one you love. It's by following him that you accept me, and make me gentle, humble, and generous!

CHAPTER 7

Representing Your Father's Interests

Social Studies was Briana's favorite subject in school. She enjoyed learning about different people and cultures around the world. Briana hoped to travel to other countries and explore the way other kids lived firsthand. Until she was able to do that though, she read tons of books and imagined herself traveling to the destinations she longed to visit.

Briana felt sad during class discussions about countries where kids experience war, hunger, and disease. Can you imagine a bomb going off in the middle of your street? Briana had even learned that there were places where people lived without running water. News like that bothered Bree and made the things she griped about seem, well . . . little. She was starting to get why her mom was always telling her to eat her food and be grateful.

Daughter, You Decide

There are people who need help in all parts of the world. If you could go anywhere in the world to help make a difference, where would you go?

She didn't know how she could do it, but she wanted to make things better. So, Briana went to the first person she always did when she needed answers—Jessica. After all, that's what best friends are for, right? The girls talked one day after cheer practice. "Jess, something's been bothering me," she said.

"What's wrong?"

"You know how we've been talking about the villages where the people don't have water and food and stuff?"

"Yeah. That reminds me, I forgot to label my map. Did you finish yours?"

"Not yet. Some of that stuff is really starting to bother me."

"It's just a map, Briana. It won't take more than fifteen minutes, tops."

"Not the homework, Jessica! The stories. I mean ... the people. Look how blessed we are, and them, maybe not so much."

"Well, I try not to think about it too much."

"That's just it; I can't stop thinking about it. I mean, can you imagine what it must be like not to be able to just go to the fridge and grab a bottle of water when you want it? Or what about not being able to take a shower after sweating all day in the sun?"

"Eww. That's disgusting."

"I'm serious, Jess. We have to do something."

"I understand how you feel, Bree. But what can we do? Nobody would take us seriously. We're too young."

"They will if we show them that we really want to help."

"Well, for starters, we have no money . . . honey. And whatever you decide to do, you're gonna need lots of that to make it work."

"You stopped saying 'we.' So, I'm in this by myself then?"

"Of course not. You know I'm with you. I'm just saying we need to think it through. That's all."

"You're right about that."

"Tell you what, why don't we talk to Michael about it? He can probably help us."

Jessica's brother, Michael, was in college, and he was the leader of a group of students who are always serving people in the community. He'd let Briana and Jessica tag along once when they were building a new home for a family whose house was destroyed by a tornado. He would know what Briana could do.

That night when they talked, he had some great ideas about how the girls could get started. "Start small," he said, "but think big. You don't have to go to another country or even another city to find hungry people."

It was hard for Briana to believe it, but Michael told her that people not less than thirty minutes from her house didn't have meals sometimes. "Are you serious?" she said.

"Absolutely. And the list goes on and on." He showed Briana a list of all the service projects his organization was working on for the school year. "So you see, there is no shortage of people who need help right in your own backyard. It's just up to you to take the initiative. So, what's it going to be?"

Briana had no answer for Michael. How was she supposed to know what to do?

Briana's Box

Talking to Michael only confused Briana. She wanted to help, but now she was overwhelmed with options! What would you choose to do if you were in Briana's situation? Wow, you really are sounding like your heavenly Father's daughter now! The first thing to do is ask Father God. Here's why.

Father God loves the people of the world. He does not want to see them destroyed. His heart's goal, or mission, is reconnection with his human creation, removing the separation that Adam caused when he got off track. You do remember Adam, don't you? Then, of course, you remember what Jesus did! Jesus is the Son who solved the problem of alienation from Father God.

Praise Prompt

Psalm 47 is a joyful picture of all groups of people praising God. As you read it, imagine how exciting it would be to dance, sing, and leap with excitement before the Lord, along with billions of other people. Now that's what you call a celebration!

Psalm 47

Clap your hands, all you nations;
shout to God with cries of joy.
For the Lord Most High is awesome,
the great King over all the earth.
He subdued nations under us,
peoples under our feet.
He chose our inheritance for us,
the pride of Jacob, whom he loved.
God has ascended amid shouts of joy,
the Lord amid the sounding of trumpets.
Sing praises to God, sing praises;
sing praises to our King, sing praises.
For God is the King of all the earth;
sing to him a psalm of praise.
God reigns over the nations;
God is seated on his holy throne.
The nobles of the nations assemble
as the people of the God of Abraham,
for the kings of the earth belong to God;
he is greatly exalted.

Yet, Jesus is not the only problem solver. God chooses other daughters and sons to become problem solvers too. Yes, that means you! Yet, you don't get to decide which problem you get to solve. Father God has already done that for you.

You would feel just like Briana if you had to decide which problem to solve. Do you remember how she felt? Overwhelmed, right! When we are responsible for solving too many problems, we do our jobs poorly. Father God relieves us of the burden of trying to do it all by giving each of his daughters and sons specific deeds that complete his mission.

In the same way, let your light shine before others, that they may see your good deeds and glorify your Father in heaven.

— *Matthew 5:16*

Still, you do have a responsibility to identify your job in helping other daughters and sons complete the mission of your Father in heaven. As one of his daughters, you represent his business interest of reuniting the world with him.

We are therefore Christ's ambassadors, as though God were making his appeal through us. We implore you on Christ's behalf: Be reconciled to God.

— *2 Corinthians 5:20*

The way you know what Father God has assigned you to do is to ask him in prayer.

Believing with Briana

Do you remember who Briana asked for help (well, besides her bff!)? A big brother, right! Just as Briana went to Jessica's big brother, Michael, you can turn to your big brother, Jesus. Like Mike, Jesus Christ had a list of things Father God called him to do. Jesus said,

> "The Spirit of the Lord is on me, because he has anointed me to proclaim good news to the poor. He has sent me to proclaim freedom for the prisoners and recovery of sight for the blind, to set the oppressed free, to proclaim the year of the Lord's favor."
>
> — *Luke 4:18–19*

In the towns and villages in which he traveled, Jesus did his part to complete the Father's mission by:

- teaching in their religious meetings,
- telling publically the good news that God's heavenly realm and authority was on earth,
- taking away every disease and sickness.

Now that's what you call good work! Are you ready to get in on the action? Your age is not a limitation. With some help from the adults in your community, you can start becoming a good leader right now, Faithgirl!

Daughter Deed

Think of your age as an asset, not a restriction, and start serving now. Girls like you can be the most compassionate and generous people in the world. Your energy is amazing! Can you do a daughter deed? In the space below, list the names of ten adults (please, Faithgirl, don't forget your parents!) that you know will help you serve in your community.

_____

_____

_____

_____

_____

_____

Look at Briana's tidbits. They share some great ideas for ways you can serve, based on the experiences you've shared with her in this book.

Briana's Tidbit #1: Host a Clothing Drive

Do you remember Briana's struggle to find an outfit to wear on her first day at Live Oak Junior High? There are many children with a much bigger problem than a new outfit for one day. Consider organizing a clothing drive in your community to help kids in need of clothing. Near to the beginning of the school year is a great time to do a clothing drive for school uniforms. Or, when the cold winter months are approaching, you could organize a clothing drive for warm articles of clothing.

Briana's Tidbit #2: Feed the Hungry

Banana-nut muffins anyone? Briana taught you a lot about a healthy spiritual diet, remember? Many people lack nutritious food to eat. Hunger is a crisis affecting millions of people throughout the world. You can help solve the problem in your area by hosting a food drive and giving the cans to the local food pantry. Or you could organize a group of parents and kids from your youth group to prepare and serve meals in the building of your local church.

Briana's Tidbit #3: Protect the Children

Briana introduced you to the adorable Foster twins, Madison and Mason, when she helped her sister, Ashley, babysit. Their parents wanted to keep them safe from the fumes while they painted the house, remember? It's hard to imagine that anyone would ever want to harm a child. Yet modern day slavery, also called human trafficking, endangers the lives of millions of children throughout the world. Many of the victims are girls your age. What can you do to help? One way is to raise money to support the work of large organizations that work to fight human trafficking. With the help of adults, you could organize a kids' night out program. Offer to provide safe, entertaining childcare for families in your community at a low cost. Then donate the money you earn to trustworthy groups fighting human trafficking.

Briana's Tidbit #4: Help the Hospitals

People of all ages dislike hospital visits. Yet, being in the hospital is a real bummer for kids. Briana's leg injury taught you just how important it is for young people to have a family of supporters cheering you on to recovery when you're sick. You can encourage a sick child by volunteering at your local children's hospital. Most hospitals would love to have you come and read to their young patients. Or you could coordinate a card-writing campaign and have your entire class, club, team, or cheer squad make bright, color- ful get-well cards to send to sick kids.

Briana's Tidbit #5: Ban Bullying

Briana's ex-cheer mate Taylor was fierce! Even though Briana understood why Taylor was hurt, you learned that violence is never an acceptable solution to a prob- lem. Still, bullying endangers the lives of countless children every day. You can help by speaking up if you know someone is being bullied, just as Briana did. More than that, you could host a rally or carnival to increase the peace in your community. Invite and include adult counselors, community leaders such as pastors, and well- known antiviolence organizations to your event.

Briana's Tidbit #6: Share the Good News

Briana's glam slam was a blast! To top it all off she got great gifts from her family and friends, including a Bible from Austin's mother. How cool was that? You can't be a Faithgirl without one! Yet, millions of people do not have a Bible translated into the language they speak. Can you imagine trying to read the Bible in German? Can you host a used book drive? Invite your family members, friends, and neighbors to donate their books. Sell them to your local book reseller, and then donate the funds to a trustworthy Bible translation ministry.

Beginning with Briana

As you ask Father God what your assignment is, he will bring more ways you can serve to mind. After praying and receiving directions from Father God, pray again! Never stop praying. Ask your parents, teachers, friends, and sisters and brothers in the family of Father God for help. Then get ready, Faithgirl! Before you know it, you'll be working with your heavenly Father to accomplish his mission!

Daughter, Declare Your Prayer

Father, thank you for choosing me to work with your Son, Jesus Christ! Help me to become the problem solver that you are calling me to be. Show me the gifts and talents you have given me to help fulfill your mission. Empower me to use them to draw people to you. I am excited about doing good deeds that honor you!

Faithgirlz Journal

My Doodles, Dreams, and Devotions

Just Between You and God

Looking for a place to dream, doodle, and record your innermost questions and secrets? You will find what you seek within the pages of the Faithgirlz Journal, which has plenty of space for you to discover who you are, explore who God is shaping you to be, or write down whatever inspires you. Each journal page has awesome quotes and powerful Bible verses to encourage you on your walk with God! So grab a pen, colored pencils, or a handful of markers. Whatever you write is just between you and God.

Other Books in the Faithgirlz! series

NIV Faithgirlz! Bible,
Revised Edition

Nancy Rue

Every girl wants to know she's unique and special. This Bible says that with Faithgirlz! sparkle. Through the many in-text features found only in the Faithgirlz! Bible, girls will grow closer to God as they discover the journey of a lifetime.

Features include:

- Book introductions—Read about the who, when, where, and what of each book.
- Dream Girl—Imagine yourself in the story.
- Bring It On!—Take quizzes to really get to know yourself.
- Is There a Little (Eve, Ruth, Isaiah) in You?—See for yourself what you have in common.
- Words to Live By—Bible verses for memorizing.
- What Happens Next?—Create a list of events to tell a Bible story in your own words.
- Oh, I Get It!—Find answers to your Bible questions.
- The complete NIV translation.
- Different covers available to reflect your unique style.

Available in stores and online!

We want to hear from you. Please send your comments about this book to us in care of zreview@zondervan.com. Thank you.

ZONDERVAN.com/
AUTHORTRACKER
follow your favorite authors